Innerbloom

Finding True Inner Happiness & Creating Your Best Life

Sarah Ordo

Innerbloom

Cover Art © Caroline Johnson

caroline-teagle.squarespace.com

Edited by Cara Lockwood

edit-my-novel.com

ISBN: 1979261237

ISBN-13: 978-1979261234

CONTENTS

"If you feel lost, disappointed, hesitant, or weak, **return to yourself**, to who you are, here and now and when you get there, you will discover yourself, like a lotus flower in full bloom, even in a muddy pond, **beautiful and strong**."

-Masaru Emoto, *Secret Life of Water*

1 | INNERBLOOM

"Innerbloom" is the name of a song by one of my favorite bands from Australia, Rufus du Sol. It is one of those songs that makes me get goosebumps all over and sends chills down my spine when I hear it playing. When I saw them live in Detroit for the first time, the song was even better in person than it had ever been over Pandora or iTunes. Not only did I love everything about the song, but I also had fallen deeply and madly in love with the name of the song. I romanticized what I thought the word "innerbloom" meant with my own interpretation of the word. To me, the name of the song makes me think of the idea of blooming like a flower from the inner most parts of ourselves, where our heart and soul are housed. It made me think about how as we grow, mature, and change we too bloom into something beautiful from the inside. This may have absolutely nothing to do with why the band chose that name for their song, but for the purpose of this book, just roll with me here.

When I try to visualize this idea of innerbloom-ing, I picture a lotus flower blooming strong and beautiful. If you know a little bit about the lotus flower, you know that it is a beautiful flower that blooms from the muddiest of waters. Something so resilient that holds so much beauty literally grows and blooms up from thick, nasty, unpleasant mud. Talk about resilience. I can't help but think that this is exactly what we do in some of our own lives. We too have the ability to grow and bloom beautifully again no matter what type of shitty "mud" we've been stuck growing out of in our life. I loved this idea so much that I've even contemplated getting a tattoo with a lotus flower or the word "innerbloom" somewhere on my body since the idea has stayed in my mind so much and for so long.

Something about this idea of blooming from the inner most parts of our hearts and souls struck a chord with me in the long run. It focused my thinking over and over again back to the idea that each and every one of us goes through our own version of innerblooming as we walk through life. This idea seemed to perfectly sum up everything I had been through in the last several years, and I'm sure many other people out there can relate this idea to their own lives as well. We've all been in the mud and we've all been stuck. But we all also have always had the ability within us to bloom again. So what happens when we bloom from the inner most parts of our hearts and souls, regardless of the muddy waters life may have planted us in? We bloom from the inside and reach our own true inner peace and happiness, which all of the world can see on the outside too.

As I write this book, you may wonder if I could possibly know everything there is to know about finding true inner peace and happiness... I am only twenty-eight years old, and no, I probably don't know everything there is to know about the topic. But what I do know is that I have done a head first jump from the high dive board into this journey of finding any and every little thing within myself and within my life that I need to be truly happy every day. I am deep in the trenches of finding everything within myself that makes me feel alive and full. I am on a relentless pursuit to discover as much true inner happiness as humanly possible. I aspire to create and live my best life every day of my life. I am on a mission to love myself more than I ever thought possible. I am determined to experience amazing things and see amazing places. I am blooming from the deepest parts of my heart and soul, and it is such a beautiful thing.

Why now? I started to realize that for years now I have been relying on the idea that once I attained certain things in my life on the outside that everything else would just fall into place naturally. Once I get that job, once my business grows, once I get into a serious relationship, once I have kids... then my life would be complete. So many ideas I had about my life started with statements just like these that were dependent on outside people or things. I thought that I needed these outside things or events in my life to take place before I could get where I needed to be. I had no idea that everything I needed to be truly happy was within my own power the ENTIRE time.

If you haven't read my first book, *Sober As F****, let me give you a little background about myself... At twenty-six years of age, I woke up in the emergency room and walked out of it alive when I really shouldn't have. I had allowed years of ungodly amounts of alcohol, drugs, and partying to finally catch up with me, and they ultimately landed me in an ambulance ride to the Emergency Room of a Detroit hospital. Three grand in hospital bills, being told I shouldn't have walked out alive, and one big fat slap in the face from life later, … I knew that it was time to change my life.

With over two years sober under my belt now, everything about my life has changed for the better. It was the hardest thing I have ever done, but now I couldn't be more grateful for it. Calling my first two years of sobriety a rollercoaster ride would be an understatement... I hit rock bottom, I slipped into depression, I let men walk all over me, and I lost many people along the way (including my own self for a little while there) because of my decision to better my life…It was an absolute SHITSHOW.

Things had to change. Something needed to shift. And I knew it. In the beginning of my sobriety I struggled more emotionally and mentally than I ever thought was possible. It showed me many things about myself and the way I was living my life. It taught me a lot about how I approached the difficult things I faced. It showed me a lot about the people I chose to surround myself with on a daily basis.

I had to get down and dirty and tear my life to pieces. I had to break through every habit, every negative thought, every little thing about my life that was not positive and supporting my well-being and start making some serious cuts and changes. It was back to the drawing board. If I wanted to truly bloom from the inside and reach my own inner happiness, I was going to have to do the self-work and the changes necessary to get myself there. It was all on me, and ONLY ME, to make it happen.

One of the biggest things I learned to do along the way in my sober journey was how to truly love myself again. For so many years of my life, I had looked outward for people or things that I thought would make my life feel full, happy, and light me up. Whether it was alcohol, material things, the approval of others, or the attention of men, I was constantly searching out other people or things to make me feel complete, to make me feel whole, and to make me feel like I was good enough. I had grown up to be so reliant on the constant approval and praise of others. When I didn't have it, I felt like something was actually wrong. This is what probably led to all of my extensive drinking and partying. When I was out there being the wild child, I got the attention I had grown to crave in life. I thought that people envied my lifestyle and that just fueled my fire. While I portrayed this confident, successful, fun, young woman on the outside, I was really just drowning all of my deep rooted issues away with alcohol on the inside. Once I didn't have the bottle to lean on anymore, I was forced to actually face all of my issues and baggage in life head on, and it was not pretty (or easy) at all.

So what drove me to write this book right now? Well, there was still one thing that I have continued to relentlessly search for to make myself feel happy and complete for years. I have been able to rediscover myself and many things that are fulfilling to me, but the dating part was still difficult. During my first two years of sobriety, I dug to the deepest parts of my heart and soul to discover what made me feel alive again. I discovered that I love to cook (and eat, of course). I uncovered a new love for fitness and my health after I had been destroying my body with alcohol and drugs for years. I learned that travel is one of my biggest passions in life, and that it gives me an indescribable "high" and happiness like I felt when I was partying. I traveled by myself and saw amazing places that filled my heart and soul up. I removed many toxic and negative people from my life. While getting sober, I was able to get down to the nitty gritty in almost every area of my life and discover what I needed within me to feel like myself and to feel truly happy again... except for when it came to love and men.

I had become so reliant on male attention and dating in life that for most of a decade, I needed to constantly be with someone to feel good about myself. During my first year sober, I was an absolute hot mess emotionally. I was in a few relationships where I let men treat me absolutely horribly. I was cheated on, lied to, abandoned, and shown that I wasn't worth it. I was so lost in my own journey of self-love and growth that I allowed all of these negative things and people to be in my life for quite some time. I repeatedly turned to dating apps like Bumble and Tinder to continue to receive the attention I craved once I stopped partying. I was so used to being at the bar and having men fall all over me every weekend. When the partying stopped and I didn't have that type of reassurance that I was good enough to others, it really started to shake my self-confidence. I spent hours mindlessly swiping through Tinder window shopping for men. This one was too short, that one was too sloppy, and I couldn't possibly be with that guy with the early-on receding hairline.

Because I felt like I needed someone else to make me feel whole again, I gave all of myself to anyone that showed that they cared the smallest bit. As long as they were attractive and gave me the attention I craved, I would turn my head away from all of the red flags that came flying high with these men. Now I'm not trying to bash these apps or say that they don't work, because I have heard hundreds of success stories about online dating. And to be completely honest, at the time I am doing my final run through and editing of this book I have met a truly wonderful man that has shown me exactly what love should be like. And you guessed it, I met him on Tinder. I had been previously online dating in the most shallow way possible. I didn't care about who they were, really. I didn't care about all of the drama and baggage that a man brought along with him. I only cared that they were physically attractive and gave me the type of superficial attention I thought I needed. I'm sure you can figure out that I wasn't choosing wisely, and my track record of the years prior to this pretty much speaks for itself... Cheaters, cowards, and liars, OH MY.

When I first started writing this book, for the first time in a very long time, I had been standing on my own two feet without someone else on my arm. I spent a long period of time truly alone, and it allowed me to really do the self-work that I had been needing to do to get to the point I am at now. So what finally got me to that point, you ask? A guy finally got me to open up to him and then played me, and he played me good. He told me everything I wanted to hear and was a great salesman in more ways than just his profession. I finally opened up again after I had built a wall taller than any wall President Trump had ever dreamt of raising up. I felt like such a fool for letting myself fall for it. It was a great eye opener to the fact that I hadn't changed my ways entirely yet when it came to dating and relationships, and I still had a lot more work to do. I did not need a man in my life if this was how he was going to treat me. I was better off on my own! (Don't worry I eventually did get his pathetic excuse of an explanation...Boy, Bye.)

I vowed at that moment that it was time for me to cut deep into my heart to REALLY deal with these issue immediately. I needed to find the love I searched for so desperately from others inside my own self before I was ever going to find it from someone else. I had to convince myself that if I found the type of love I needed one day down the road with someone else, great. But from that moment on it was going to be all about ME.

I deleted every app, turned down every guy from my past that continued to contact me, and truly was ALONE for the first time that I could remember in years. Was it lonely at times? Sure. Did I miss the 'Good Morning' texts from a new guy I had just met? Sure. But what I was gaining during this time alone was a newfound confidence like I had never felt before. This time I wasn't just putting out a front and posting bullshit motivational quotes about being happy single. I finally was reaching that place for real. And it felt freaking AMAZING.

I began to recognize what a strong woman I was capable of being. I began to acknowledge all of the things I have accomplished in my life. I began to realize that I was a truly amazing individual and a woman unlike any other woman on this Earth. It was at this time that I began to truly appreciate and love myself again from the deepest parts inside of my heart and my soul. I was truly happy. Not fake smile and going through the motions happy, but truly, deeply, and authentically happy.

The crazy thing about what has happened is this... Once I began to pull away from the outside people, things, and relationships that did not add to my life in a positive way and did the self-work that was needed, the things that I wanted and needed were attracted to my life like magnets. Once I began to look inward rather than outward, I reached a point of inner peace and fulfillment that I truly cannot put into words. Life felt full, my anxiety was quieted, and my fears simply started to melt away. I did the hardcore self-work I had been needing to do for a long, long time. I practiced the self-love I had been needing to give myself for a long, long time. I began to look at everything in my life in a new way and with a new purpose. Once I started doing this, every little thing just started to make more sense. When I stopped searching for things, they began to find me. It was like every little piece of my puzzle began to fall from the sky and into my life. The Universe was releasing each one of them with insanely accurate timing. Only when I completely stopped looking outward and did the inner work did the things I needed and desired begin to be drawn to me naturally.

But one of the biggest things that I have been able to do by looking inward is learning how to let love in again. I've had a hell of a track record when it came to dating and men. Cheating, abandonment, lies, abuse, manipulation... you name it, I put up with it in my past. This led to my building walls, avoiding relationships to avoid getting hurt, and never completely letting anyone in. When I was so lost during the early days of my sobriety, I was not the strong, independent woman I had always prided myself on being. I had lost her and morphed into this weak, desperate little girl laying myself down on the ground to let others almost trample me alive.

While I was stuck being so reliant on finding someone on the outside, I wasn't thinking about what I needed on the inside. I wasn't allowing my heart and my soul to truly heal. I wasn't focusing on ME. This had led to depression, no self-worth, and allowing myself to be used and then thrown in the garbage. I needed to wake up, open my damn eyes, and find that strong girl deep down inside of me that I knew was somewhere inside still hiding out. She needed to come back out and take center stage. I needed to identify the things I wanted and deserved to find in a partner. I needed to set boundaries of what and who I would allow into my life in the future. If I was going to let anyone into my life again in a romantic way, they had to add to my new life I was building in a positive way. They would need to love me for all that I am and have been. They would need to add to this amazing transformation I was going through to be the best version of myself while creating the best life for myself.

So right now I've come back to edit this part of the intro because as I have been working on this I can feel something shiftng within me. I initially started this book thinking I'd be writing about how to be a badass, strong, independent woman that doesn't need anyone but herself to be truly happy, at peace, and full of authentic self-love. I expected to rant on and on about how you don't need a man and/or a woman to be happy or complete. I will probably still write a part of this book like that, because I still believe everyone can be truly happy on the inside whether they are single or taken. But, wouldn't you know it, the Universe seems to have other plans for me. Something I had been looking for for SO long on the outside has been drawn to me, but only after I started looking inward and loving myself first. I stopped looking for it. I pulled away from everything, I focused on myself, and I redefined the things I would allow to happen inside of my own life. I redefined the boundaries of what I would allow to come into my life and what I deserved to have be a part of my life. And the craziest thing has happened now... I've let love in again for the first time in a long time.

It was only when I reached this place of truly appreciating my life and loving myself again that things have been able to get to this point. The place I am at now is one that every man and woman deserves. I live each day in a way that makes me love everything about every day of my life. I have created a life for myself that is full of true inner happiness and love. I no longer only look forward to certain things in my life, now I look forward to every day and the opportunity it brings to truly live and be happy.

Of course, there are always going to be bad days or unfortunate things that happen because that's just life. But I cannot explain to you how amazing it feels being able to know that even the bad days are only there to make the good ones feel that much better. There is always an opportunity to make things better. There is always an opportunity to experience more happiness. There is always a way to feel more love. I wake up each day feeling truly empowered and full of possibility. There will never be a limit of how much happiness, peace and love I am capable of bringing into my life and my heart, and the thought of that it absolutely thrilling.

So, yes, at the time of finishing this book, I have finally been able to let love in again. First from myself, and now from someone else. It was not until I reached true inner happiness and love within my relationship with myself that I was able to have it with someone else. Rediscovering the woman I am and loving every inch of myself was the first step in getting there. Rebuilding my life in a way that promoted true inner happiness and peace every day was what I needed to do to transform the way I was living. Finally reaching the place in my life that felt happy, calm, and full was the ultimate goal.

SARAH ORDO

You never know what the future will bring, but right now at this point in my life I have reached the best place I've ever been able to reach. I am confident in myself. I am proud of my sobriety and the journey I fought through to get here. I am so in love with someone who has truly shown me what love should really be like. I am sharing life with some of the most amazing friends. I am walking this new journey with one foot in front of the other, and I have no intentions of slowing down or changing the direction I'm going in one bit. I almost lost this life and the chance to feel this way once before, and I won't ever take it for granted like that again. I now feel more alive and present in my own life than I ever have before, and I want to live, breathe, and feel every single second of it to the fullest extent possible every single day that I can.

I feel so truly alive, happy, and at peace inside, and I think that every person deserves to feel this way too. No matter how much shit you've been through, no matter how much you've screwed things up, and no matter how much you might try to resist it, YOU deserve to feel this way too. You deserve to live each day with a happy and open heart. You deserve to live each day with a smile that wears naturally and cannot be hidden, even if you tried to hide it. You deserve to be open to every good, positive thing in the world that could come your way. You deserve to feel love again in the truest and most authentic way possible from yourself AND from others. You deserve to feel true inner peace and happiness deep down to the deepest parts of your heart and soul. You deserve ALL of it… and don't you ever forget it.

So my idea behind this book it to share the process and journey that helped me find happiness again by turning my sights inward. If I could cut myself open and look deep inside to figure out what makes me feel truly alive, then you can too. It won't be easy at times, but I can promise you that it is SO worth it. The journey I went through was full of ups, downs, twists, and turns. There were times I just wanted to throw in the towel and walk away. There were times I was just plain tired. There were times I just wanted to give up completely.

Use the goal of feeling happy, content, and full as your reason to keep working at it. Think about the place you could reach at the end of it if you just keep going. Think about how amazing life could be if you let it. Think about what your best life would look like, one that is truly happy and full of love, and turn that into your finish line and destination.

To be honest, this journey will never be entirely done because what fills you up and makes you happy can change multiple times over the span of your lifetime. We change so much throughout our lives that finding our best life may be something we do over and over again numerous times. What fills you up now may change in a week, in a year, or in a decade. I've only been alive for twenty-eight years so far, and I can personally say I have been a chameleon shifting and changing what makes me happy an uncountable number of times. Partying, alcohol, and superficial attention used to be what I thought made me feel alive and happy. Today, I could not be farther away from finding true inner happiness in any of those things.

Finding out what makes you tick inside is a never ending journey because the evolution of yourself throughout your life never reaches an end point. Think about how exciting it is that we can tweak and recreate our best life over and over again. We can constantly be looking for the next thing we want for our life to make it even more amazing than it already is… to make it even more full than it already is… to make it even more overflowing with happiness and light than it already is.

Once you are able to identify and discover the things inside of you that make you feel truly happy and complete, you will be able to cut out the things from your life that are unnecessary for you. You will be able to walk away from the things that no longer serve you. You will be able to identify things that are no longer good for your well-being. You will make the changes you need to make to better yourself. You will stand with open arms welcoming in the things that make your heart feel full. You will search out the things that make you feel alive. You will strive to fill your life with only the best things and people every single day of it. Hey, you might even let love in again.

Let my words and my journey be your road map, but feel free to take as many detours as you need to. Your path to finding the destination of your own true inner happiness won't match mine exactly, but I can guarantee it will share a lot of similarities. We're going to cover a lot of areas of your life in this book and you're going to be challenged to look at them in a pretty cut-throat way. You're going to be challenged to change or remove many things in your life. You're going to be asked to look at things in a whole new light. You're going to have to really cut through a lot of bullshit if you want to truly change your life for the better.

As you go through each chapter, try to really focus on the area of your life that we are going over. Try to look at things from an unbiased place and in a completely neutral way. Look at your past and also at your current place in life. You may have already made some of the changes you needed to make to better your life, and you hadn't even realized it yet. Keep going. Keep moving onto each new chapter and each new idea. Use what you read to analyze your life, how you are feeling at that very moment, and to start identifying what you need to do to get to the place you want to be. Highlight things that strike a chord in your heart. Circle things you want to focus on and remember. Mark pages you may want to come back to and go over again. Take notes at the end of each chapter about what you discover along the way. YOU'VE GOT THIS.

Investing time in yourself and being truly happy will be more valuable than you can ever fathom. It's going to take work. Its going to take deliberate effort and change. It's one hell of a journey and a whole lot of work if you want to create a life that is truly full of happiness, peace, and love. It's one hell of a process to truly bloom. The journey is long and never ending, but one of the most rewarding and fulfilling ones you will ever embark on in this lifetime. Pinky swear.

THINGS TO REMEMBER:

_____

_____

_____

_____

_____

_____

_____

_____

_____

_____

_____

_____

_____

_____

_____

_____

_____

_____

_____

2 | WAKE UP

How long have you been going through life looking for others to fill up the spaces in your heart? Do you rely on getting a buzz from alcohol to have fun? How worried are you about the opinion of others? When is the last time you had actual "me" time? Ask yourself these questions right now, at this very moment in your life. When you reflect on how much of your life you have probably spent looking outward rather than inward for happiness, you can really start to feel like a weak-ass bitch… Sorry, but it's true. When I first identified how much of my life I had spent being so desperate for external and material things on the outside to make me happy on the inside, it made me feel shallow and hollow. It made me feel like I was weak and desperate. I realized that for so long I didn't carry the confidence within myself to not need any of these outside things to feel complete. I have a feeling I'm not the only one who has been living this way for a big portion of my life. How many of us are guilty of constantly looking for someone or something on the outside to make us feel true inner happiness on the inside?

Now don't get down on yourself just because I said we are weak-ass bitches. Everyone starts somewhere in their journey of self-growth and self-work, and this is where we will start ours. Wanting for people and things on the outside to make us happy is what we have been trained to do for years, so it is only natural that that is what we all do out of habit. It's easy and it's all we know. Unless you had super awesome hippie parents that taught you to love the Earth and yourself and that you don't need material or external things to be happy, odds are you are one of us. So until we can actually acknowledge that we are looking outward for all of our happiness in life, we won't think we are doing anything wrong at all. It's just how we've always gotten through life.

We present ourselves to look perfect on the outside to feel confident on the inside. We envy and strive to reach the success that we see others achieve in their lives to make us feel successful in our own lives. We wish we had that tall, dark, and handsome man as our husband to make us feel worthy and loved as a woman. We wish we were happy with any and every aspect of our lives. We question ourselves daily on how we are supposed to actually achieve this. We might even question IF it even possible to actually achieve it at times.

While we are striving to reach that place of true happiness on the inside, we are often relying primarily on the outside factors in our lives to get us there. Sure, attaining and reaching some of these things may help us out a little bit, but those things can't always tackle the job of inner happiness entirely on their own. They might give us that temporary fix for now, but just like when the shiny new iPhone X gets dropped and we immediately think we HAVE to have it, we will always be looking for the next best thing to answer all of our problems again. We will just keep repeating the vicious cycle of thinking that maybe something new and shiny will finally make us happy if we aren't truly content on the inside first.

So how have we grown to automatically look outward to find these things rather than inward? Well, first, let's take a look at social media... Every picture on your Instagram feed is showing us how to lose weight, how to have perfect hair and makeup, and how to be "happy." Don't even try to tell me you aren't following people on

Instagram because you love to look at their lives in their perfectly posted and edited photos. Traveling to exotic locations, having a ridiculously attractive boyfriend or girlfriend, and perfectly staging a photo of their Acai Power Bowl they had for breakfast next to their latte with the little intricate foam design on top. Just to rub salt in that wound a little bit more, let me tell you that that same person with millions of followers probably got paid hundreds of dollars just to tag the coffeehouse that made that latte and hashtag them in the caption. Welcome to the world of modern day social media marketing. THIS is why we think our own lives aren't good enough, because our lives don't look this perfect in our own personal photo album on our cell phone. Our albums are full of photoshoots of our dog sleeping in the most adorable positions, the parking section number we parked in so we don't forget where our car is, and 25 failed selfies (one of which is probably an accidentally front-facing camera selfie that just makes us want to give up on life altogether).

We are spoon fed the idea that perfection on the outside equals happiness on the inside in every day of our lives. Marketing the most ideal, perfect lifestyle to the public makes each and every one of us want to do what we see other people are doing and buy what other people are buying. Don't lie, just admit it. We've all been envious of what someone else has or is doing in their life. We have all been there at some point. It is human nature. We want what others have. The neighbor's grass always seems to be greener when we look over the fence into their yard. We want perfection, we want happiness, and we have grown to believe that attaining these outside things in our lives will give all of it to us. The truth is that you can spend a whole lot of time and money attaining lots of things and still be absolutely miserable. Money may buy you some happiness in life, but it surely can't buy you all of it.

I can't even begin to tell you how many times someone in my family has drilled me with questions about how or why I was still single. "When are you gonna meet a nice boy and settle down?" and "When are you going to give us grand babies?" are questions that have dominated the conversations of my mid-to-late twenties on the regular. It's like every old-fashioned minded person resonates with an idea that something is wrong with us if we are alone. Even my mother would constantly compare my and my brother's still being single around the age of thirty to all of her friends who have grandchildren already and ask why we haven't done the same yet. Lay off me Mom, I'm busy being a "Boss Babe," okay? When I subtly remind her how many things we have both achieved and accomplished in our young adult lives, don't worry, she totally changes her tune. I may not have a baby yet, but I do have a self-published book... (#micdrop).

Although we are challenging the idea more than ever before, there still sometimes is this strange stigma that has been around for a while about girls being destined to be wives and mothers. Thank God we are starting to challenge this norm, because there is a whole lot of awesome stuff out there to be accomplished by women in the world (sorry, boys, but it's true).

Even though we are challenging the norms for women everywhere, I can guarantee that many of the women (and men) reading this have felt the pressure a few times in their life to be looking for "the one." Once we meet that guy or girl everything will just fall into place, right? It may... but it also may not. With our biological clocks ticking (especially us, ladies), we often feel the urge to find someone more and more with every day that passes. It's not right or wrong to do this. It's really somewhat normal in a lot of our minds. If we see ourselves being parents, husbands, wives, and having families, then we are definitely going to be looking for our significant others in life to some extent. We don't live forever and our age definitely can put the pressure on when it comes to starting a family when we feel we should (or are supposed to).

I know that as the big 3-0 draws closer and closer there were many times I stopped and thought about how I had always said I wanted to have my first child by the time I turned thirty. Why? I'm not sure, really. When you are young, I guess something about thirty just sounds like a rite of passage in age. The closer I get to it, it really doesn't seem so old to me anymore.

So, as I neared the end of my twenties, I will admit that there have been times I've felt a little panicked about the idea that I hadn't even found "the one" yet being so close to thirty. I've just had to accept the fact and face the music that the things I planned to have by thirty might not happen exactly the way I always thought they would. I've even told myself in the past not to panic about having children, because I could always adopt or use a sperm donor if I didn't meet the right person at the right time. That's right, I had literally thought that far ahead already. Come on, people, my twenties are ending and I can hear the biological clock ticking louder than ever! Really, I just want to have children and I am an extremely impatient person. I know I have plenty of time still and am being a little bit ridiculous, trust me. It has just always been a dream of mine to be a mother, and I wanted to make sure that I didn't miss out on that just because I didn't meet Mr. Right during a certain time period of my life. If being a mother is what I desire in life, the amazing thing about the world today is that I can do it all by my damn self if I choose to (with a little help from someone's else's sperm, of course). Talk about an amazing and empowering time to be a woman in the world, right?

We are all constantly striving to make more money every day thinking that if we have an overabundance of it that surely our problems would fade away. Well, tell that to celebrities like MC Hammer and Sinbad who have each made millions of dollars and were still forced to file bankruptcy when things in their life quickly went south. Have you ever watched any of the reruns of good old "Behind The Music" on VH1? As the Notorious B.I.G. once told us, "Mo Money, Mo Problems." Sure, money can buy you lots of sparkly, shiny things. Money can take you to lots of fancy places. Money can give you the illusion that you can attain anything you want in life with some crisp Mr. Benjamins. But can money really make all of you happy down to the deepest parts of your heart and soul? After seeing celebrities go through multiple stints in rehab, extramarital affairs, and seeing the sad occurrences where some of them have even taken their own lives, I really don't believe at all that money can make you truly happy. Money can buy you a whole lot of stuff, but it obviously can't buy you true inner peace and happiness all on its own.

We say yes to so many things because we feel we have no other choice. We take on way too much work when we are already feeling overwhelmed. We want to take care of and fix others who do not show us the same love and care in return. We feel like we constantly need to be working on or accomplishing things to feel like we are doing enough. How many of these things that we feel obligated to do are really filling up our hearts? How many of these things are feeding what we crave deep down in our soul? Some of them might, but what about the things that do not? I am going to challenge you to identify these things and ponder what would happen if you just started to say "no" sometimes. I dare you to start saying no to the things that serve you no purpose in your life. If they do not benefit your well-being and your happiness and it won't hurt someone else by not doing them, then start saying NO. But more on that topic later.

Are you loving yourself? Not just living with yourself on the day to day lifestyle you currently have, but actually truly LOVING everything about yourself and who you are. Your skin, your weight, your personality, your hair color, your company... Are you confident in yourself physically, emotionally, and spiritually? Are you comfortable spending time alone? Do you ever spend time alone?

I absolutely hated being alone for years of my life. I hated spending an evening watching tv by myself, and I hated going places alone. I was not comfortable with just the company of myself at all for a long time. I wasn't fully loving myself and who I was, and I needed to acknowledge and work on it, big time. If you haven't taken the time in life to really focus on self-love, this area is going to be HUGE for you. Loving yourself can change so much about your life and your well-being than you probably ever realized was possible. Well, get ready, sweetheart, cuz there's about to be a whole lotta love coming up in here.

Mindset is going to be everything along the way in this journey. Your thoughts control everything about yourself and your life. While you cannot control a lot of the outside factors in your life and how they influence the course of it, your mind frame and your thoughts can. You can't always control what happens to you in life, but you can absolutely control the way you respond and act in response to them. Knowing this will be CRUCIAL to rolling with the punches that are inevitable in life. You can work to ensure that your thoughts and feelings don't sabotage your growth and progress in life, and in this journey to inner happiness. When it comes to your mindset, you have both hands on the steering wheel always whether you are aware of it or not. We're going to start making sure that you're steering in the right direction on your own personal journey from now on.

We're going to heal. We're going to truly heal whatever it is inside of you that may be holding you back. Shitty things happen to us in life. I'll be the first to attest to that idea. It's how we comeback from them that matters. If you let the set-backs keep you held back, they're going to cause bigger problems.

We're going to look at the opportunity to use the hurt, the mistakes, and the screw ups to propel us into an opportunity to turn them into something new and better. We're going to view negatives as an opportunity for positives to take shape. The set-backs set you up for the comebacks, and everyone loves a good comeback story. You probably aren't even aware of how some things that may have seemed so small in your life may have left HUGE, lasting effects on how you've been living. Let's dig deep to identify these things and take away the power they have over you so you can bounce back and get your bloom on again.

We're going to make everyday a little more special. We're going to basically work towards bursting with positivity in all areas of your life at all times. Wouldn't it be amazing not only to look forward to certain days and events in the week to week grind, but to look forward to every single day instead? Wouldn't it be great to not constantly be looking at the clock for the day to end? Wouldn't it feel awesome to not constantly be looking forward to the weekends when you don't have to be sitting at a desk all day? Think about how nice it would be to look forward to every day in life, not just certain ones on your calendar.

We are going to focus on some outside things along the way in this journey too, of course, but only the ones that enhance our inner self and well-being. These outside things can play a huge role in contributing to our inner happiness, no doubt. Like I said earlier, unless you are going to live a minimalist lifestyle, you're still going to be dealing with some external things that can assist with your inner work. You can't avoid some of them altogether, so it's just going to be about focusing on them and deciding what things are going to be best for your heart and soul on a regular basis. The things that don't contribute in a positive way, we are going to cut away. We just need to figure out what they are, if we truly need them, and what we can replace them with that is more positive instead.

So, at this point, I dare you to cut away all of the shiny, sparkly things that catch your eye. I dare you to cut the cord with the people you feel you need to make you feel whole. I dare you to say NO to the things that do not bring you joy. It's time to start changing your life. It's time to live the most positive, best life possible every single day. It's kind of liberating to think about it, isn't it? What if you and I truly cut through and cut away all of the external bullshit that we think will make us happy and figured out how to be TRULY and authentically happy on the inside?

It's time for us to WAKE UP. Here's your little pep talk to get you all hyped up and ready for what we're about to do. We're about to shake up life and make it bigger, badder, and better. It's time for us to get down to the bottom of what makes us feel fulfilled, complete, and whole. It's time for us to truly look inward instead of outward for our happiness in life. No more reaching for things on the outside in an attempt to resolves all of the problems we have within our lives. It is time for us to look inside of our own hearts, our own dreams, and our own souls… And that's exactly what we're about to do here.

Our daily lives have been so focused on looking outward rather than inward because that is the easiest thing for us to do. It's the instant answer. It's the quick fix. It is what we naturally want to do out of habit. It's what we've always known how to do. Nobody wants to do the hard work most of the time if they are given the choice not to. It's always more appealing to take the shortcuts. But not here. Not this time.

It's when we start to look inward for the things we need that it's going to take more work. We're not taking the easy road with this one. It's easy to always be thinking that once you get the guy, buy the house, or have those 15 minutes of fame that you will finally feel the way you've always been wanting to feel inside... happy. It is easy to look out at all of the things you want or feel you need and place a lot of personal value on them. It is easy to think that once we have these things in our own two hands that things will just simply make sense. To me, this sounds like trying to find the instant answer to all of the challenges we face in life. Just like going on a crash diet to lose weight, it may give you that quick fix, but it usually also won't give you a lasting result. It's the hard work, the slow and steady approach, and the lasting lifestyle changes that give you the long term results you have been wanting to see. So let's get 'em.

HERE WE GO. What do you strive for in your life? What are the things that make your heart feel full? What are the things that make you feel complete? What does authentic inner happiness look like to you? What kind of people do you see as enhancing your day to day life for the better? We're about to dive head first into the journey and self-work of finding out what our personal true inner happiness looks like.

I wouldn't call it "work," really, and you might realize why right away. It can actually be super enjoyable when you make yourself a bigger priority in your own life. It's time to make yourself a more important part of what you focus on, so put yourself up on that pedestal IMMEDIATELY. We're basically going to fall in love with ourselves, spoil ourselves, heal ourselves, and recreate ourselves into the newer, bigger, badass-er version of who we used to be. Pretty exciting stuff, huh? If you're not excited yet, well... get excited!

It's time to turn our sights inward rather than outward to discover what makes our hearts beat faster, our smiles grow bigger, and our souls feel more alive. It's not always going to be easy and it's going to take practice and deliberate work, but it is time to look for the things we can find WITHIN us rather than OUTSIDE of us. Your body, your skin, and your bones house every little thing inside of you that you could ever need in this life to feel whole. Your heart and soul harness the capability to reach that place of inner happiness, inner peace, and so much love. You might not be at the point where you believe it yet, but I bet we are going to change that attitude of yours real quick.

It is time to wake up, open our eyes, and start our journey back to true inner self love, peace, and happiness... one step inward at a time. Hope you enjoyed this little pep talk of ours. Now, ready, set, GO.

THINGS TO REMEMBER:

_____

_____

_____

_____

_____

_____

_____

_____

_____

_____

_____

_____

_____

_____

_____

_____

_____

3 | SEASONS OF LIFE

Spring, summer, fall, and winter... undoubtedly these are the first things that come to your mind when you think of what seasons are. Depending on what region of the world you live in, these may vary for you a lot. As the different seasons arrive, things change naturally and inevitably. The temperature changes, what time it gets dark changes, and of course, Pumpkin Spice flavored everything comes out seasonally, too. Even though I love a good PSL from Starbucks, let's focus in on roses and just how the seasons affect them and their blooming. Do you walk outside in the morning to the frigid winter morning air and stop to smell the snow covered blooms? Impossible. What happens to the beautiful, strong, resilient rose bushes once the temperatures drop and the seasons shift? Just to be a little extra, I decided to lay out some of the things that one must do when winter comes to prepare and ensure that the rose bushes survive the cold, frigid, dark winter to bloom strong and beautiful again in the spring...

Depending on the climate and how low the temperatures will drop, the process varies on exactly how much precautionary work you must do to protect the roses and prepare them for the coming winter. The roses will naturally form "hips" or seed pods in preparation to protect themselves for the winter season. A basic step you must take is to cut and prune back the roses and remove any canes that are overly long to prevent further damage or strain on the plant. By cutting away the longest parts of the plant, you allow it to use its energy to regrow these parts even stronger later on. Some climates suggest covering the actual rose bush above the dirt with a Styrofoam cone, cardboard box, burlap, or bales of hay to provide it shelter as it endures the winter season. In some very cold climates, it is even suggested to dig up the roots of the plant completely and dig out a trench in the soil to completely cover the entire plant to bury and protect it from the coming frost, ice, and frigid temperatures.

Once the frost breaks and the spring season begins, the rose bushes begin to grow back again, but only when they are ready and only when the conditions are just right. They show their resilience as the bush itself begins to grow back the previously pruned canes that were dead and cut off. Buds will then begin to form in preparation for the blooming to happen again. Once the timing is right and the air reaches the perfect temperature, the bush reblooms. The rose bush blooms again just as stunning as ever before. It's strong canes with sharp protective thorns lead to each individual rose… Beautiful, resilient, and strong with each soft, delicate petal it reveals as it opens itself to the warmth and the sun.

You've probably already picked up what I'm putting down here with the whole roses thing. There are seasons of life for us just as there are seasons of blooming for roses. Most flowers do not bloom year round, but rather flourish during certain times of the year, just as we do throughout certain times in our lives. There are certain conditions in life that enable us to bloom strong and beautiful like the roses in spring, and then there are other times that life and the things that come along with it naturally want to hinder us from blooming, just like the roses in winter. Just like rose bushes, WE go through seasons of bloom over and over again throughout the course of our lifetime. How many times we will go through them is absolutely uncontrollable. Our entire lifetime can really be seen as a cycle of blooming and reblooming numerous times. It is natural and we have no real power over it. Just as we cannot stop the seasons from changing throughout the course of the year, we cannot stop the seasons of our own lives from coming along just the same.

When the conditions are just right, we bloom with all of the strength and beauty we can contain within our own human bodies. These conditions are all about positivity, nourishment, and love. When we feel supported and loved, we bloom. When we feel confident in our own bodies, we bloom. When we accomplish things that carry great meaning to us, we bloom. When we reach true inner peace and happiness, you guessed it, we bloom.

Think about a time in your life where you feel like you were "blooming" and showing your inner most happiness and beauty on the outside that you also felt on the inside. It may have been when you accomplished something great. It may have been a time when you felt truly beautiful. It may have been when you welcomed a child into the world. It may have been when you discovered your calling in life. It may have been overcoming whatever it is or was that you consider to be your own personal season of "winter" in your life. If you take a few seconds to think about it, you can probably think of at least a few times in your life when you felt like you were truly blooming with authentic inner happiness from the inside out.

When I reflect on the past few years, I can identify some definite seasons of bloom in my own life. Reaching milestones in my sobriety were times that I felt I had come through the "winter" of my own life and come back strong and beautiful. Being able to proudly share these milestones with the people in my life just made me bloom even more. But the times I felt like I bloomed out of control have been when I've realized that I have the power to share my story and help others through their own personal "winter" in their own life.

As I opened up to the world and allowed people into my journey of sobriety and rediscovering myself, I felt more strong, resilient, and full of beauty than I ever have before. I felt true inner happiness and peace down to the deepest parts of my heart and soul. I was in full bloom and absolutely nothing could bring me down in those moments. Sharing my first book has been the peak of my blooming so far in life. I have a feeling that I will definitely feel that same way again once this book is completed and released as well. When I put my heart, soul, and emotions into something and send it out into the world for others to share in it, I am absolutely in full bloom. When I am in full bloom, I have the most true and authentic inner happiness absolutely bursting from the seams! It is always hard to describe what it feels like inside when you are just truly happy with every single tiny fiber of your being. I've grown to crave it over and over again since I first discovered how truly amazing it feels.

When you are in bloom, you show all of your beauty and strength again to the world. You show that you have gone through the seasons to get there. You are showing that you have traveled down the paths to get there. You are showing that you have done the work. You are showing that you can always come out on top. You are not hidden away to protect yourself. You are open. You are on full display. You are showing the world everything you've got inside of you. You are showing the world that you can do some amazing things. You are being strong yet vulnerable, and proud yet humbled. Think of it like the rose blooming after another harsh winter, the lotus flower blooming through the thick muddy waters, or like a phoenix rising from the ashes. Invincible. Unstoppable.

When a person blooms, there is nothing quite like it. It is a time of strength, beauty, and resilience. Just as we admire a stunning bouquet of roses, people may be admiring you in the same way when you bloom. You will just have that something about the way you walk, the way you talk, and the way you go about your days. It will totally show when you are in a season of personal bloom, and people may stop to admire the beauty of YOU when you bloom. So let them stop and smell the roses.

But just like the rose bushes, it is important to also remember that we too are not intended to bloom at ALL times and during all seasons of our own lives. You are going to have bad days and hard times, and you are ABSOLUTELY allowed to have them. They are unavoidable. You are going to have dark, cold, frigid "winters" in your own life. There is going to be struggle. There are going to be harsh conditions that you must endure and get through. Times are going to get rough. Things are going to go wrong. Shit is gonna get hard. That is just the path that life goes down. It is impossible to have everything go right 100% of the times. Absolutely impossible. If we had that much control over what happens to us and in our lives, we would all be on a cake walk down easy street. But that is impossible. So you must accept that you will have "winters" in your own life to have a healthy view on things overall.

In reality, I like to think that our personal "winters" are the times that really build us into the people we will grow to be. Although they suck when you're in the middle of them, they cause you to work and fight through something adverse. They cause you to come back stronger and better than before if you want to get out of them alive. They give you the opportunity to bloom again. They also give us time to hibernate and rebuild for our rebirth come spring. I like to think that my winters make me appreciate my blooming in the warm, bright, happy times even more. Without cold, dark times would we even appreciate the good times as much as we do? Your winter is there for a reason. Trying to grasp this idea will make it much easier to take what we can get out of them and get through it.

My winters… oh, man. There have been many winters in my own life. Some were short and quick, while others seemed to pull me in with no intention of ever letting the sun shine again anytime soon. My first year of sobriety sometimes felt like one long, never-ending winter when I think back on it. Sure, it was not all dark and cold, but there was a whole lot of those types of feelings during that time. Those times tended to overshadow any signs of a warm, bright spring ever coming back. It was easy to feel hopeless. It was easy to let myself slip in depression from time to time. It was easy to let my anxiety get triggered by my weaknesses as I rebuilt myself and my life. It was easy to fall into those self-destructive, negative patterns that kept me from reaching my next season in life. But I had to fight through them. I had to protect myself from the cold, frigid things that surrounded me so that I would make it back to the warm, uplifting times when I would be able to bloom again and be happy down to the deepest parts of my heart and soul. I knew that the next season of my life was coming, I was just extremely lost and confused while I was trying to find it.

When the conditions are not favorable for our blooming, we must take the measures necessary to prepare and protect ourselves as we do the rose bushes. If we do not give ourselves the things that we need to survive and move forward, blooming again will seem near impossible. Just as we protect the rose bushes, we need to protect ourselves too. Give yourself the things you need to nurture your heart and soul. Feed yourself the things you need to feel nourished. Give yourself time to rest and recharge. You will need your strength to bloom again strong and beautiful once your winter had passed, so taking care of yourself is an absolute MUST.

This is exactly what I did while I was deep into my own journey of finding true inner happiness within myself again. I had to retreat during my winter. I holed up in my townhouse and vegged out with myself. I didn't go out as much, I spent way more time alone than I ever had before, and I did the self-work that I knew I needed to get done. I still made time to be social and see friends, no doubt. But my new priority was becoming the best version of myself that I could possibly reach. I took care of myself, I focused on my physical and emotional health more, I poured my heart out into my writing, and I watched a shit ton of Netflix. I pulled away from my normal habits and patterns that I had been so comfortable with in the past and put myself in a new and uncomfortable place. I was finally protecting myself from the self-destructive patterns of my past so that when my winter ended, I would finally be able to fully bloom again and be happy. I was finally listening to myself and what I needed to move forward and be a strong, resilient, happy young woman again.

So while you are in your winter, take the time to fully process and understand it. Why is it happening? What led to it happening? What caused the conditions of winter to come upon you? Do the self-work here, and I promise it will teach you so much. When I am able to fully understand why something is happening in my life and why I feel the way I do about it, I can come out of it stronger and more knowledgeable. When I identify how I've let things on the outside affect me on the inside as much as they have, I try to turn inward even more. I really try to acknowledge and identify what's happening on the inside and on the outside simultaneously.

What happened in our life on the outside that caused or triggered these internal feelings and emotions? Is it something someone else did that we responded to? Did we do something ourselves that triggered our own response? Have we done things to sabotage our own progression and happiness in life? Remember, this whole book is not only about finding a place of true inner happiness, but it is also about recognizing the patterns and ways we have been (or are currently) preventing ourselves from reaching it sometimes. Sometimes we are our own worst enemy when it comes to preventing our own happiness, and we may not even realize it.

I repeatedly pushed myself back into my own winter with alcohol, drugs, and men. I was pushing myself into my own winter with toxic friendships and relationships. I was pushing myself into my own winter by not acknowledging and dealing with my underlying feelings and emotions for most of my life. I never realized I was even doing this, but now when I look back I can see it crystal clear. I was the root of a lot of the problems and negative things that were happening in my own life. I was living in ways that attracted mostly negative things, people, and energy into my life repeatedly.

I eventually brought my coldest, most frigid winter onto myself, and there was nobody to blame but myself and the way I had been living my life. I had been stuck in a vicious cycle of just being absolutely lost when it came to loving myself. I was struggling in an alcohol-fueled routine of attempting to discover who I really was inside, and I was really just pushing myself farther away from finding true happiness. The season of my life where the temperatures dropped their lowest and I was in the darkest winter possible started the day I ended up in the hospital. Because of my behavior and the negativity I brought into my own life, I caused myself to end up strapped to a stretcher in an ambulance. I caused myself to risk losing everything. It was the day I almost lost my life.

Lord only knows that the fact that I walked out of that season of my life alive must have meant that there was going to be one hell of a summer meant to come my way soon, right? But I knew deep down that it was only going to come if I did the work and made the changes I needed to make in my life to welcome it. I was responsible for bringing the sunshine and the warmth back into my own life. I was going to need to bring back the soil, the water, the sun, and any other little thing I needed to support my own blooming again come spring and summer. And I knew that is exactly what I had to do. It was all on me, nobody else was going to get me there but me, and I f***ing did it.

Just as a rose needs soil, water, and sunlight to bloom, we too require certain things to support our own blooming. So take care of yourself and give yourself any and every little thing you may need to ensure that you can bloom again. Give yourself the Miracle Grow that you need to bloom. Pull the weeds. Tend the soil.

I make sure that I am taking care of myself inside and out. I nourish my body with food and water. I give myself rest.

So hibernate and prepare to endure your own winter, knowing that spring will always come at the end of it. Look at the way you are feeling during the cold, dark season of your life and listen to your body, your mind, and your soul.

If you really pay attention, you can feel and hear your body telling you what it needs. If you are feeling depressed, you may need to seek more positivity or even the help of a therapist (I absolutely SWEAR by mine for getting me through difficult seasons). If you are feeling sluggish, you may need exercise, a better sleep schedule, and wholesome food. If you are feeling lonely or isolated, you may need quality time with friends and loved ones. Do the work. Give yourself the things you need. You too can make it through your seasons with resilience, you just need to be there and do the work that is necessary.

I can personally say that once I started looking at my life as a series of "seasons" it became SO much easier to accept the fact that you can't stop things from happening. Whatever you are going through will always pass. Even when it seems like you are stuck and there is no light at the end of the tunnel, time will always go on. Life will always go on. Tomorrow will always come. Whatever is meant to happen is just going to simply happen, and you can't stop it. It's like that saying that everyone always says that "whatever is meant to be will always find a way." You cannot stop things in your life and hit the pause button because things will always continue to move and progress and change. Just like you cannot stop the progression of the seasons, you can't stop the progression of your life either. Learning how to roll with it and adjust to various situations and outcomes is the best way to get through life. It will make it a much smoother ride and keep you from completely losing your mind.

So do not ever get down on yourself for not "blooming" 24/7. It's very easy to think that because you don't have a perfect life where everything goes right that things are hopeless. It's easy to think that maybe you have failed it things aren't shiny and spotless. It's easy to surrender to the hard times and the difficulties in life. Being weak to your own personal winter is the easy approach, but it offers little reward. You will just get stuck there if you let yourself. Keep reminding yourself that the cold season of your own life leads to the warm, light, sunny times that are always following it. Embrace your seasons. Take what you can from them, and use them to better yourself in the long run. Life experiences are sometimes the greatest teachers and learning opportunities, so take everything you can from your seasons and use it to learn and grow.

Your winter will probably bring some bad days. So if you need to have a bad day, embrace having a bad day. I literally have a little pity party for myself and allow myself to bask in the shittiness of my bad day funk of a mood when I come upon one. I do this only with the mindset that it will pass, just as the seasons always do. You've just got to get through it. And you will. If you need help, ask for it. If you need to change things in your life, change them. If you need to take a little time to figure it out, then take your time. Pull through your own personal winter any way you have to so you can get back to the point where you can bloom again at the end of it with happiness and love. That's the whole reason why you picked up this book about finding true inner happiness in the first place, right?

I'm sure there have been some amazing times in your life where you wish you could hit pause (or at least the slow motion button) so that you never forgot how happy you were and how great things were at that time in your life. You always want to feel that warm, feel-good happiness rushing through your body. Maybe it was the day you fell in love. Maybe it was the day your son or daughter was born. Maybe it was a vacation in the most beautiful place you'd ever seen. These are the times we want to always feel. Feeling this way and experiences true happiness makes us want to avoid our undesirable seasons altogether, because who wouldn't want to feel freaking amazing all the time like that?

Think about some of the times in your life that you'd like to hit fast forward and get the hell out of ASAP. Times like these could include deaths of loved ones, horrible breakups, struggling financially, etc. Getting out of those negative times and yucky feelings as fast as possible would be pretty nice, huh? It would be so much easier just to get the hell out of them as fast as we can then to have to actually feel all of those negative emotions and feelings inside. Unfortunately, we know that things just don't work that way. So, if we can't get rid of the winters of our lives altogether, we can at least change the way we approach them and think of them. But we also need to realize that we can actually USE our undesirable seasons of life to learn from them in unlimited ways.

This idea of using our undesirable winter season to learn and grow from it is an idea I'd like to discuss further. I touched on the idea earlier on in this chapter, but I want to stress more how we can always take some positives out of our winters no matter how bad they are. If anything, we can learn from what brought the cold, dark times upon us. We can see what we want to do differently or what we may have misjudged in our winter and use them to gain knowledge. Did we do anything to cause this season to happen? Did we allow something into our lives that triggered it? By looking at the situation from this viewpoint, we can go forward knowing that we don't want to repeat some of our past actions again. We can go forward knowing how to handle certain situations and relationships better. We can go forward realizing certain people or situations need to be removed from our lives. We can go forward knowing how we want to feel in our lives, and what we need to do different next time to get there. There are so many valuable lessons we can take out of our dark, cold times in our lives moving forward, so try to USE your winter if you are upon one.

During my winters, I was able to learn what I did to bring them upon myself. I learned that certain people brought them on as well. I was able to see what triggered my anxiety and depressing. I learned what affected me in a negative way emotionally. I used what I was going through and experiencing to gain knowledge moving forward. If I was going to be stuck in a shitty season of my life, I was going to get something good out of it in the long run no matter how I had to do it. I knew there had to be SOMETHING that could be taken from even the most negative experiences. That one golden little nugget of knowledge that I could take away from it and use in a positive way. Call it my optimistic, glass-half-full outlook on life... but it worked.

By looking at things in a more optimistic, positive way, I learned how to pull myself through and/or out of a winter. I figured out the things I needed to give myself to survive the cold, dark times. I learned what changes were necessary in my own life to avoid them more often. I realized that within myself I had the power and ability to change ANYTHING I wanted to about my own life. I cannot tell you how valuable it was to realize one day that I harnessed all of the power necessary to pull myself out of an undesirable season and bring myself right into a new one. THIS HAS BEEN GOLD. And you have that power within you, too. You may not realize it yet and you may need to figure it out as you go, but you absolutely have it within you too. Believe it.

So as we move on into the other areas of this book, keep in mind the main ideas from this chapter about the seasons of our lives and our "blooming." We are not intended to bloom year round. Seasons will always change and we cannot stop them. Take care of yourself any way that you have to in order to ensure that you will bloom again in your next desirable season. Give yourself the things you need to survive. Embrace your winters. Learn from your winters. Stay positive. Stay optimistic. Realize that you harness the power within you to get through and change ANYTHING in your life. You are a rosebush, surviving the winters to bloom strong and beautiful again every spring and summer.

THINGS TO REMEMBER:

4 | THE SKIN YOU'RE IN

What do you see when you look at a happy person? Most of the time a bright, shiny smile, an ease to everything they do, their head held high, and a totally positive presence. Happy people tend to just ooze self-confidence. Do they look at the floor, kick at the dirt, and mumble to themselves underneath their breath? No. Their heads seem to always be high with those confident smiles plastered across their faces proudly. They walk with good posture, a powerful stride, and a sense of security in themselves. You can tell when someone is not confident and in love with who they are in life. If you are not happy and confident with every inch of yourself, inside and out, you're going to struggle with true inner happiness. There's no way to bullshit or sugar coat this one. Insecurity and low self-worth will only hold you back, limit your well-being, and keep you from living your best life possible. Every. Single. Time.

If you are not confident in yourself, why would anyone else be confident in you? Honestly. If you are constantly doubting yourself, others will probably start to doubt you too. If you are constantly getting down on your weight or your appearance, you're asking others to focus on your body in the way you negatively see it, not for its true strength and beauty. If you doubt your ability to nail that project at work, the boss might not see you as the first choice for big assignments anymore. What you feel and what you show others you feel about yourself will always influence what they see when they look at you from an outsider's perspective. If you doubt yourself and who you are in the skin you're in, others won't see all that you have to offer inside of your heart.

First of all, let's just be honest and address the fact that EVERYONE has struggled with being confident and secure in their own skin at some point in their lives. Especially us, ladies, in all of our stages including the awkward puberty stage… Changing body shapes, learning to shave, and getting your first period, oh my. Then we go through childbirth and that comes along with a whole other slew of body changes as well. It's not always easy being a woman when it comes to our bodies. We put them through the ringer, that's for sure. Don't get me wrong, what the female body is capable of doing and creating is absolutely a blessing and incredible, but it does affect our bodies and the way we look in big ways too. I think we can all relate that sometimes it's hard to adjust to all of these body changes that happen throughout life.

So, yes, we all struggle about things involving our changing bodies in life at some point. Everyone wants to be young, pretty, and thin. Have you ever stopped to take a minute and really look at the health and beauty industry? I work in the thick of it, so I'll be the first to tell you… We are selling people things and ideas to convince you that you want to do anything and everything you can to make yourself look younger and prettier. Bottom line. Buy this weight loss shake. You need this foundation to make your skin glow. Get lip injections to make your lips fuller. It's kind of sad when you really think about it. In a way, we're often telling you that you need to buy this stuff and do these things to change yourself to look better and feel better about yourself. It's superficial and shallow, but we're all guilty of doing it.

First of all, how many of us have been on "diets" throughout our lives? I've done them, too, don't worry. Lean cuisine frozen dinners, 90-calorie "brownies" that taste like dry dirt, and don't even get me started on Slimfast shakes. Many of us have resorted to these quick fixes to give us an instant weight loss and confidence boost. We are all constantly fixated on the idea that "once I lose those last 10 pounds..." everything is going to be a-okay. A number on a scale should never be a deciding factor on how happy you are in life and with yourself. All I'm gonna say is Kim Kardashian has killer curves, a huge ass, and cellulite when she wears a bikini, and she's living the life of her dreams right now because she just OWNS IT.

Plastic surgery is such a normal thing now that most people just change whatever it is they don't like about themselves just like that. Now, I'll be the first to admit that I'm not against getting a little filler in my face one day if I decide I would like to try it out. I wouldn't mind some nice, fuller lips. Never say never. There are some people that are so truly unhappy with things about their physical appearance that having a procedure done finally makes them feel confident in their own skin. I actually remember a girl I went to high school with that planned for years on getting a nose job because she absolutely hated her nose. She got it done, it looked great, and you could tell she was SO much happier with herself. So, I throw no shame on it. You've gotta do whatever makes YOU happy. You gotta do you, boo boo. Just try not to get too carried away and come out looking like you have duck lips and a monster face. Please!

So why don't we focus more on taking care of ourselves and our bodies rather than what we think is wrong with them a little bit more. Let's try to shift the focus on embracing what we have rather than fixating on what we wish we had. You'll look better, you'll feel better, and you'll see lasting results. Treat your body as a "temple," as corny as that sounds. But really if you think about it, we were given this one body and it was designed to do amazing things for us. This body was made to pump blood throughout us, keep us breathing, make us feel things, allow us to do miraculous things... This body we have is literally capable of creating and growing another human being inside of it. That's INSANE. We get this one incredible body that carries us through everything we do in life. We might as well appreciate it and show it some love in return. We only get one body, so you better take the best care of it that you can.

Focus of taking care of yourself. Get enough sleep. Eat nourishing foods. I'm not saying to give up burgers and pizza forever (because hell no!), but think of food more as fuel. Everything in moderation, that's my motto. Take care of your skin. Wear sunscreen. Exercise. Drink enough water. Get a facial or a massage. I guarantee that if you start taking better care of your body you will just start to feel better all around. Do things for your body that make you feel good. Feeling good will show on the outside as you begin to feel more happiness by simply taking better care of yourself.

Getting comfortable in my own skin has been a journey throughout the years. When I was younger and took ballet and dance classes, I would only eat cans of lima beans or dry cereal until dinner on some days to make sure I kept my daily calories down. I did the usual cycles with Slimfast shakes and meal replacement bars on and off throughout my teen years. I've always been a really tiny girl (I'm only 5 feet tall), but I've always had curves. I blame it on my accepting my unavoidable love for carbs, but I've grown to LOVE this body. Have you seen how many songs have been written about booties alone over the years? Embrace them curves, girl.

I have always stayed regularly active and worked out since I was a teenager, but with a totally different mindset back then. The reason I worked out in the past was to look good. I wanted to look good in my scantily clad, whore-ish outfits at the bars and clubs every weekend while I was slamming back shots. I wanted people to think I was attractive and want me. I had a very warped image of self-worth back then, if you didn't already figure that out. So I worked out to make sure that all of the empty calories I guzzled down in the form of alcohol and taco bell every weekend didn't cause me to gain weight.

I've obviously come a long way as I've gotten sober and changed everything about my life, and taking care of myself has been a huge focus. I no longer obsess about what I eat. I no longer obsess about doing cardio to stay thin. I've started doing the things I need to do to FEEL good, and in turn, it causes me to look and feel strong and healthy. Looking strong, healthy, and confident in myself is way more attractive than being super skinny and strapped into a skin tight body con dress so short that you might flash your leopard print thong when you try to get out of the car (like Britney circa 2007).

To keep my body strong and healthy, I do regular workouts that incorporate running and weights, and weights have pretty much changed my life. I have never seen how strong my body could be. I'm definitely not ripped, but I can see my muscles grow and my strength shine through. It makes me feel incredible. If you have not stepped into the world of weights yet, I suggest you try it. I promise you won't blow up into one of those steroid-pumped guys at the gym walking around in muscle tanks. I'm actually toned for the first time in my life! I used to just do a straight 45 minutes of cardio and be done with working out. I finally had someone teach me how to work out using weights and strength train the right way. Now, I spend half of my workout time doing strength training, and my body feels better than ever. I am stronger and more toned, and I have more energy than ever before, too.

I try to also eat healthy, nourishing foods the majority of the time now… But if I'm going out to dinner and I want pasta, you know I'm getting pasta. I'm also going to hit that bread basket… HARD. Like I said, everything in moderation. I don't go into a carb coma at every meal, but I also don't deprive myself of things I enjoy if I want to indulge a bit. If you deprive yourself of something you want, you're only going to put it up on a pedestal and want it more. And then you will probably end up binging on an entire loaf of bread with seasoned dipping oil at some point… It's all about balance.

Do you ever notice how you can start to feel sluggish and

uninspired at life when you lay around in pajamas all day? Do you feel the sugar coma after downing an entire bag of dark chocolate? Do you constantly make empty promises about using that gym membership? Start changing the way you look at your body and how you take care of it. Start making small changes to make your food more nourishing for your body. Look at food as fuel to keep that body pumping and moving and doing the incredible things it was intended to do.

You don't need to jump right into being a Crossfit pro immediately either, but start moving on a regular basis. You'd be surprised by how much a little exercise a few times a week can totally change your mood, your outlook on the day, and the way you feel. Check out the local gym. Take advantage of that one free training session that comes with the membership there. Try a fun outdoor yoga class with a friend.

Accepting the things we consider to be "flaws" about ourselves is a HUGE step in finding true inner happiness with the skin we're in. I bet most people reading this can name at least one thing you would change about yourself if someone asked you right now. There's always going to be things about us that could be more "perfect" if that's the way we are looking at it. For years I had said that I HAD to get a nose job when I turned 18. I am Russian and I have very distinctive facial features, including a nose that I always thought was way too big for my face. The fact that I broke it and it got a bump on it when I was a teenager just made me feel the need to change it even more. I used to bitch and complain about my small chest. I always thought I needed to lose five pounds and that my thighs were too big. I always wished I was taller than five feet, too. Why are we always so stuck on changing things about ourselves to be what is probably just someone else's made up version of what "perfection" looks like? There is no definition in the dictionary that says perfection is 5'9" with long hair, a tiny nose, and a D-cup bra size.

Accepting the things you consider to be your flaws can just take plain old time, but it IS possible. Flaws are what make us unique. Flaws are what make you, YOU. What makes us different is what makes us who we are. If we were all tall, skinny, blondes with perfect boobs things would get pretty boring out there. Every skin tone, every body shape, every type of hair are all unique and created for each person they suit. We are meant to be unique and one of a kind. Once we can begin to fully acknowledge and accept that, things will get a whole lot easier. Embrace every little thing you consider to be flawed, because it is what makes you who you are in the long run. It is what truly sets you apart from the crowd. And how amazing is it to think that no one was created just the way you were? You are literally one of a kind to the truest extent.

The amount of self-respect I have gained for myself as I have accepted everything about the skin I'm in is an extremely powerful thing. As I grew to accept the things I always considered to be my flaws, I gained such a sense of strength and respect for myself that I wouldn't let anyone hurt me or threaten my well-being anymore. With the respect that I have gained for myself, I no longer let people try to come against me or hurt me. I do not let people that can't see all of the beauty I have to offer come into my life in a close or intimate way. This has been extremely evident to me in dating. Having this newfound sense of pride in myself has made me "un-****-with-able." Any man that has not shown me that they see all of the beauty and strength I have within myself does not get to stick around. This newfound strength and respect has enabled me to no longer settle and to truly hold out for the people I deserve.

Once I finally got comfortable with myself, I no longer obsessed with wanting to change things about me. This is how tall I will always be. My small boobs are perky as shit and show no signs of sagging anytime soon. My bigger hips and thighs give me killer curves in a body con pencil skirt. I could obsess day in and day out about the things I wished were different about myself, but accepting them has been a way easier route to take.

The skin you're in is a gift. Like I said earlier, you were given this incredible body, which was built piece by piece to house your heart and soul. It enables you to do every incredible, amazing thing you will do in this life. So take care of it. Appreciate it. See what it can do. Push yourself. Don't scrutinize and break down every little thing about it. This body of yours is an amazing vessel, and it can take you anywhere you want to go and enable you to accomplish every little thing you want to do.

It takes time to get to the point of loving every inch of your skin for most people. For myself, I know it got much easier as I got older and matured as a person. It got MUCH easier with plain old age, to be honest. Somewhere towards the end of your twenties I feel like you just become a lot more comfortable in your own skin. You realize the things that really matter and the things that kind of don't matter at all in the big picture. And that tiny bump in my nose… well, it also was along for the ride when I've accomplished and achieved some of the greatest things in my life so far.

You will be able to accomplish big things whether you lose those last 5 pounds or not. Someone will fall in love with you whether you have big thighs or not (they may even LOVE those thighs of yours, girl!). You will have amazing friends that won't care if you're getting your first signs of wrinkles on your forehead. In most situations, nothing about your body or the things you consider to be "flaws" will keep you from reaching the places you want to reach. Flaws will not keep someone from loving you. Flaws will not prevent you from getting your dream job. Flaws will never prevent you from having lasting friendships. These things we focus on about ourselves will never have the power to keep us from being happy and living our best lives unless we let them. If you give them too much power, they can absolutely prevent you from being truly happy and living your life to the fullest. So, let's NOT do that.

I have seen some of the most inspiring people in life that have truly overcome their flaws or things that were different about them and gone on to do amazing things. I went to high school with a guy who was born with Prune Belly Syndrome which affected him physically in many ways. He has gone on to do amazing things and even started his own foundation, despite the things about his body that make him different. There are competitive athletes with missing limbs that are absolutely incredible at what they do. While these are examples of big things that people have overcome to flourish and be successful in life, I hope that you can relate it to your own situation in your life in some way. Any little things that you think might not be perfect about yourself can never hold you back. You must be able to overcome the things you view as flaws or differences and crush them so that they have no chance to limit you in anything that you do.

It is important to realize that nobody has given flaws a place in your mind except for you. Flaws only get real power when you let them become something. Flaws aren't real things, they are ideas and ideals you have created after you've compared yourself to something or someone else. Or maybe they are ideas and ideals you have created after someone else has criticized you personally. First of all, nobody is perfect and nobody ever has the right to ever criticize the skin you were born in. Please try to refrain from ever giving them the power to do so. But I will say it again, flaws are not real. They are ideas. WE have created these ideas. WE have given life to these ideas. WE have given power to these ideas. WE are the ones that can either allow or not allow them to influence our happiness and the way we live our lives.

Let's switch the focus over to confidence. When you give off a vibe of self-confidence, you ooze strength, beauty, and self-worth. You show others exactly just what you are worth to yourself. As I mentioned earlier, can't you just tell when you see someone walking around with confidence? You can literally see it in the way the walk, the way they talk, and the way they act. People want to talk to confident people. People want to be around confident people. Single people in the dating world are drawn to confident men or women. Their energy is contagious. They encourage and invoke things in the people around them by simply being in their presence.

Being self-aware and knowing exactly who you are and what you have to offer is a very strong thing to possess. Being secure in what you look like, what you do, and how you live your life can be incredibly empowering. Being able to show the world who you are exactly as you are takes a LOT of strength and self-confidence. To get to the point where you are no longer trying to hide, play down, or change things about yourself should be the ultimate goal here. True and authentic confidence in ourselves in every way possible.

How do we gain more self-confidence? First, we already discussed how we need to just send our "flaws" to pack their bags and get out. Next we need to focus in on the good things about ourselves. What makes you special? What makes you unique? What are you good at? What do you offer that nobody else can? Every single one of us has strengths, talents, and gifts that we can be confident about. They may be small or big. They may be a million different things. Regardless, everyone has something about themselves that can be celebrated.

By focusing and spotlighting our greatest features, talents, or assets, they start to take center stage. With a little bit of intention, you (and others) can begin to always highlight your best features in everyday life and everyday situations. By focusing on the positive, we stop focusing on what we think is the negative. We're literally training our mind (and the minds of others) to look at the good things first. If we continue to keep highlighting the things that are positive about us, we will continue to reduce any power that the negative thoughts may have. It will start to seem like second nature to be effortlessly confident when you are always putting the best parts of you on the foreground for everyone to see.

I've caught myself being someone in the past who has lacked a little self-confidence at times. It's not unheard of and pretty much all of us have done it. I realized that as a teenager I used to look down at the ground when I walked past people sometimes. I doubted myself when something I wanted to do seemed like it was too big or too hard. I have let others judge me and get down on me and carried their words with me long afterwards. I didn't even realize I was doing it at the time, so you may have done it in your own life too and not realized it. I think a lot of us do it out of bad habit. A lot of us have probably been used to experiencing some criticism and judgement in many areas of our everyday lives without even being aware of it.

Most recently, I can relate this to my starting to write and self-publish books. I am a pretty motivated, go-getter type of a chick, so I set my mind to doing this and I was going to get it done any way I had to. But when I started to let my mind wander to what I could grow these books into, I felt myself feel overwhelmed at times.

I would think something like "What if I could start a website with all of my content and books and videos for people to visit? I could update it regularly with tons of videos and blog posts…" As excited as the idea would sound, I would feel myself allow anxiety and a sense of being overwhelmed to creep in when I really started to think about how much work it would be. When the thoughts would start to race about how I possibly could accomplish all of it on my own I had to stop myself. If I focused on the negative things about the situation I was going to doubt my ability to do it, one hundred percent. I wasn't showing the confidence I know I have in myself and the things I can do by thinking this way.

When I found myself slipping into that mainframe of feeling unconfident and anxious, I shifted my thoughts. Rather than focusing on how overwhelming and how much work it sounded like, I focused on all of the things I have already accomplished that I never would have imagined I could have done. Focus on the positive. Focus on the things you HAVE done. Oh, by the way, I totally did create that entire website all on my own (and it wasn't as overwhelming as I had tried to convince myself it would be). I have battled my way through two and a half years of sobriety. I have shared my story with the world. I wrote and self-published an entire BOOK! When I focus on all of my accomplishments, somehow that confidence just creeps right back in and takes over right where I need it. When I highlighted and focused on the amazing things I have been capable of doing in my life my confidence came back doubled. With that confident mindset back in my mind, the big ideas and dreams didn't seem so overwhelming and stressful anymore. I was confident again in my ability to do the things I put my mind to.

What can you highlight about yourself? What can you focus on that you have accomplished in your life? Maybe you are a kickass stay at home mom that packs the BEST lunches in your kid's class. Maybe you started your own small business from your kitchen table. Maybe you beat depression on a regular basis. Maybe you help people in need every day in your career. Maybe you are a single parent killing it out there on your own. There are so many things you are good at. There are so many positive things about you that make you special. Put the spotlight on them and focus on them. While you're busy shining the light on those things, you will be leaving anything negative in the shadows of darkness. Let's leave them there for good.

If you are someone who is shy, has low self-esteem, or is introverted, this one may be something you will find difficult to do at times. My best advice to you is to just do the work and "fake it till you make it." I've followed that motto in several areas of my life. If you put out the front that you are confident and secure in yourself, others will believe it. If you aren't sure how to be confident all the time, fake it. You'll probably learn over time that you already knew exactly how to do it all along. If you are willing to do the work, you'll get there. It might not happen overnight. It might take a lot of getting used to. But anyone can get there.

When you truly accept every little thing that makes you who you are and realize that this idea of feeling less than, insecure, or "flawed" has no real power over you unless you let it, you will be unstoppable. When you learn to live everyday with confidence and feeling secure in yourself, everything good about you will shine in the spotlight. Being comfortable, confident, and happy in the skin you're in will play a huge part in creating your best life possible every day. Do the work and keep practicing day in and day out. It will transform your mood, the way you think about things, and the way you go about every little thing that you do. We aren't even in Chapter 5 yet and I bet you're feeling inspired and empowered as hell already, right? Keep going and turn the page. But just a heads up, we're about to get deep.

THINGS TO REMEMBER:

5 | WHAT DO YOU NEED TO HEAL?

So, if you picked up this book there is a very good chance that there is something in your life that you want to work through, change, or moved passed. We don't seek out personal development and self-help books just for the hell of it people. There's a reason. There might be something you've been holding onto that causes you pain or anxiety inside. There may be resentment and anger you are still harboring towards someone else that leaves peace elusive. Someone may have hurt you. You may have hurt yourself. You may be taking your first steps of looking inwards and doing some serious self-work to just better your life in general. Either way there is probably some healing that needs to be done regardless of the reason you started reading this book. Everyone has things from their past, people from their past, or traumas they have endured that leave long term effects on them and how they live their lives. I dare you to try to find one person in the world whose life has been spotless, shiny, easy, and perfect 100% of the time. Impossible. Shit happens. Life happens. We all have a past and we all carry baggage around from the things we experience in our lives. Period.

First of all, I want to applaud you for picking up and opening this book. The bottom line is that if you found this book and felt the need to read it, there is something in your life that you want to change for the better. You want to better yourself. You want to better your life. You want to find true inner happiness within yourself. So, kudos to you! You're already going in the right direction and have your mind set with positive intentions. Remember along the way that time spent investing in yourself and your well-being is NEVER time wasted. It is one of the greatest investments you can make in life that will reap the highest returns in the long run (unlike that Rosetta Stone CD set you bought off of an infomercial to learn Spanish but never actually listened to). This work will leave lasting effects on you that will better everything about your life.

Healing takes time. As much as it sucks, it's very true. I just heard a lyric from the country song "Every Little Thing" by Carly Pearce the other day that sings about how time is the only thing that truly heals something that hurts. It elaborates on how sometimes something hurts so much that it's unimaginable to endure the time spent trying to heal and move forward from every little memory. So the song is obviously about getting over a heartbreak, but the same idea can also apply to what we're talking about here. Unless you have no heart and zero compassion or feelings in life, healing is going to take time. It's going to be a bitch. It's going to hurt. I know we wish we could all just shut off our emotions inside and let things go, but sometimes we just simply can't. We need to feel the hurt. We need to process the things that have happened to us. We need to accept them to overcome them and move passed them.

Things happen and we hurt because we are human. It's as simple as that. We have feelings that are easily bruised and lives that are easily affected by others, especially those we care about. God, or whatever Higher Power you believe in, created us to be these amazing beings that live, breathe, and FEEL everything. We have these big, pumping hearts that are meant to feel every little emotion in our lives… from love to compassion to jealousy to heartbreak. We were carefully and intentionally designed and created to feel ALL of it. See it as a blessing or as a curse, but we are intended to feel the highest highs and the lowest lows of every emotion there is to feel in a lifetime. Some of the feelings may not always be so pleasant, but some of them can be the greatest things you'll ever experience.

We can try as hard as we can with all of our might to resist bad feelings, but when something hurts us… it hurts. Hurting can take a toll on you emotionally, physically, and mentally. It can literally cause you to feel physical pain and stress. It can keep you from a good night's sleep. It can keep you from being able to relax. It can make it impossible for you to let others in authentically. It can prevent you from growing and progressing as a person, and in your life. It can cripple you and make it near impossible to even go about your usual daily routine. The bottom line here is that when we are hurting it can influence our entire lives no matter how much we try to not let it do so.

When something triggers you, like hurt, pain or traumatic events, it can bring every difficult feeling and every difficult emotion you harbor inside of yourself to the surface… all at once. And it's not pretty. Ask anyone that suffers from depression or anxiety and we can tell you first hand, you can't just snap out of it. I can personally attest that pain and trauma in my own life have triggered some of the worst anxiety attacks I've ever experienced. If you've never felt what it feels like to have an actual anxiety or panic attack, it's not pleasant at all. Your heart races uncontrollably, you feel like you can't completely catch your breath, you pace and possibly shake uncontrollably, tears may start to pour out, and your thoughts go to a million hopeless and helpless places at a speed of a million miles per hour. You feel like you can barely function and like you are going insane all simultaneously. It is crippling and absolutely exhausting. Being triggered by current (or past) hurt can take you there in a heartbeat over and over if you do not deal with it in a healthy way at some point down the road.

It's time to look inward and identify the hurt or pain you are carrying with you. If you have had significant hurt in your recent years you will probably be able to identify a few people or situations that have hurt you greatly right away. When I think of some of the obvious signs of hurt and trauma in my life I can immediately name several off the top of my head. The biggest source of hurt I carried for a long time was directed towards myself. I carried a great amount of pain and guilt for my past problems with alcohol and the hurt I caused others because of it. I also carried a lot of pain from some of the things that happened to me while I was blacked out drunk. I can immediately identify several men that caused me significant hurt in my life by cheating on me, deceiving me, and abandoning me. I can also immediately pinpoint a particular friendship that took a turn for the worst and is now nonexistent that really tore me up inside. These are the easy ones to identify. The big guys are the ones you can name off the top of your head easily. But there are usually a lot more... so keep going.

Keep digging. There are probably things in your life that you harbor pain from that you didn't even realize caused you such trauma. Thankfully, I was able to easily figure these things out in therapy in the beginning of my sobriety. I seriously recommend therapy to everyone for this reason. Whatever hurt may be holding you back could be something from your childhood. It may be something a parent or family member said or did that has stayed with you in your subconscious for years or even decades. It may be the deception of people you thought you could trust. There can be a million different sources for the deep, hidden pain or hurt you have carried throughout life.

A lot of my deeper, hidden hurt came from negative things that were said to and about me by people I trusted or loved in my past. The struggle to always look happy and perfect when things were going wrong was another hidden source of hurt in my life. From a young age, I had been trained to always seem perfect and without flaw on the outside no matter what was going on inside. I'm sure I still have much more hidden hurt deep inside to dig out, but it simply takes time to dig up all of it. I fully expect to unbury a few more things as my life continues.

Accept the things that have happened. Accept the things that you have been carrying with you. Not dealing with things and pushing them away is not healthy AT ALL. Trust me, the emotional baggage that came flooding out when I didn't have alcohol to drown it away anymore was so overwhelming at times that I wasn't sure how to even handle it. I felt like a complete and total nut job.

Pushing things away and not accepting them will only make them continue to grow deep down inside of you. They will continue to influence the way you live, the way you feel inside, and so on. Pushing hurt, pain, and trauma away and not dealing with it like it never happened will only leave you feeling stuck, vulnerable, and helpless. It will block any chance of reaching true inner happiness within yourself. You must acknowledge the things that have hurt you. They probably suck, and I am SO sorry that you had to go through them. I wish I wouldn't have had to live through some of the hurt in my life, but I can't change the fact that those things have happened. We can't go back and change the past, so we must begin to accept it.

Accepting and acknowledging the hurt and pain you harbor within yourself is the first step to being able to move beyond it. By acknowledging these things they become REAL things that we are able to understand and grasp, metaphorically speaking. Once we are able to fully identify these things, we can start to better understand them. If you don't identify or point out the things that have affected you, you will have a very hard time trying to move beyond them and heal from them. That is why it is so important to dig deep and acknowledge the things you have been holding onto. Even the smallest, tiniest things that you might think are silly and not important can be the things that end up leaving the biggest scars.

Feel all of the pain they have caused you. Throw yourself a little pity party for about five minutes and let all of the hurt be realized. Feel bad for yourself for a few minutes and even scream or cry if you need to. Maybe even write down a list of all of the things that have hurt you that you carry inside. Put them all down on paper. Write a letter to someone that has caused you strong feelings of hurt or pain in your life. Write down how they made you feel. Let all of the pain, the hurt, and the emotions rush to the surface all at once. Feel all of the pain and let it become the power that pushes you forward. Let every feeling, thought, and emotion come through onto that piece of paper. Scream. Cry. LET IT ALL OUT.

Now take that piece of paper with whatever you wrote down on it, and f***ing DESTROY it. Cut it into pieces, rip it to shreds, light it on fire (but please don't accidentally burn down your house)... do what you need to do to physically destroy this list of things you have been carrying with you. Face the pain. Face the hurt. Then, destroy it. Let this be a visual representation of the work you are doing inside. We are destroying the things we have carried with us. We are doing the work to move towards no longer allowing the things that have hurt us to continue influencing the way we feel or live in our everyday lives.

You probably had no idea how much the pain, hurt, and trauma, of your past can, or possibly already was, influencing your life without your ever knowing it. Now on the outside looking in, I can identify that the things people said about me that destroyed my self-worth at a very young age can be directly reflected in the way I had little to no respect for myself when it came to dating and men. People that should have been positive, supportive examples of men in my life said things about me before I was even in high school that were degrading and horrible. Young men I socialized with as a preteen spread sexual rumors about me throughout the hallways of my school. It was almost like I believed the things that were being said about me. I was young and I didn't know otherwise.

In the thick of it, I had no idea that I was letting the things being said about me influence my feelings about myself. These negative feelings I harbored about myself stuck with me for a long time from a very young age, and it showed in how I was letting men treat me.

This was me and this was how I always lived my life. This was all I knew. This was what I believed about myself inside for a long time, so how would I have even known any differently? Now I see that when my self worth was destroyed at a young age it was also temporarily destroyed inside of me. I would continue to carry that with me through life until I was able to identify it and realize that is was not the truth about who I am at all.

This, ladies and gentleman, is a perfect example of how the hurt we carry with us inside can influence everything about our lives. It can influence what we believe about ourselves. It can influence the actions we take on a daily basis. It can influence our inner most feelings about ourselves. THIS is why it is so crucial to identify the hurt or pain you are dragging behind you like a rolling suitcase. If we just continue to keep dragging it behind us, it will continue to consume the way we are living. It will be near impossible to do the work to find inner peace and happiness in our journey until we are able to identify and detach from these things. It's time to cut them free.

I'm going to stroke all of our egos a little bit here, but everything I am about to tell you is one hundred thousand percent true… You are amazing. You are a unique, one of a kind creation in this Universe. There is not one other person in existence that is you. Nobody can do what you do. Nobody can be YOU. That idea right there is amazing in itself. That whether you believe in God, the Universe, or any other Higher Power, each and every one of us was created on purpose and for a purpose. You were intentional. You can achieve anything you work hard and put your heart into. Nothing is impossible for you. You are limitless. People are lucky to have you in their lives. People love you. People would be sad if you were not here anymore.

So, I know that just sounded like a thousand Pinterest boards of pretty, motivational memes rolled into one, but that was the point. To boost up your ego and convince you that you are f***ing amazing. Why? Because in order for us to let go of hurt and pain we need to first realize that we are NOT what others say or do to us. We are so much more than that. We are these incredible, limitless human beings that CAN find everything we need within us to be truly happy. It does not matter what other people have said about us. It does not matter what other people have done to us. We were created to be these individuals with our whole lives ahead of us to do whatever the hell we wanted to with them. When you were born you did not carry the hurt of a neglectful parent. You weren't born with the inability to ace that exam. You weren't born destined to stay in an abusive relationship. You weren't born with the automatic destiny to fail at things. You were a fresh start, a blank canvas, and the possibilities were endless. Pretty cool, right?

The things that have molded you into the person you are in the place you are in now are all of the external things in your life. The words, the experiences, and the people you have encountered have molded and shaped you into who you are today. They have influenced everything about your life without your even knowing it. Unfortunately, we will all experience pain, hurt, and trauma along the way. It's inevitable. Even if you tried your hardest to avoid it and your parents tried their best to protect you from it, it happened. They may have been things like a death of a parent or sibling. It may have been abuse from someone you trusted. It may have been being bullied at school for being a little different than the other kids. It could have been that backstabbing friend in college you thought you could trust.

The things that hurt you may have been big things that caused unavoidable pain. They also could have been small things that stayed hidden away in the back of your mind for years. Pain, hurt, and trauma can take all shapes, forms, and sizes. They can be obvious and they can be sneaky and hard to identify. We all have had these things happen in our lives, it's just a matter of how much they have affected us along the way that varies from person to person.

People hurt other people in their lives because they have shitty things going on within themselves, and that is the one hundred percent truth. Whenever someone does something hurtful or maliciously towards me, I try to take a minute to remind myself that they must be going through something shitty in their own life and are lashing out and taking it out on others. Does that make it okay? No. But it helps to look at it from this angle so that you can keep yourself from wanting to unleash a flood of curse words in their direction or daydream about wanting to punch them in the throat instantaneously. So I'm going to give you a mindset for how to handle people or situations like this, but maybe don't say it to their face because they might absolutely freak out in reaction to your hippie chick response to their current instability. Tell yourself, "I feel sorry that they are having to behave in this way because of their own inner hurt."

You know what we are going to do next? SAY THAT TO YOURSELF. See how crazy and nasty they just looked for taking their inner pain and hurt out on others? That is exactly what we have all been doing this entire time, but only to ourselves. We have been self-destructing our own happiness and inner peace by letting the shitty things in our lives and in our pasts control how we are living, and we probably didn't even realize we were doing it. I totally just mindf***ed you on that one, didn't I? I actually just mindf***ed myself with that one as well to be honest. It's funny how in an attempt to write things to teach others, I often end up teaching myself things along the way too. Sometimes, playing devil's advocate and being able to see things from all angles can be a blessing and a curse. In this case I call it a blessing, because we can use it to teach ourselves a valuable lesson in how we are living in our own lives when we are able to put ourselves in someone else's shoes or see things from another person's perspective.

In order to start healing, we need to first acknowledge the pain, hurt, and traumas in our life. Next, we need to dive head first into dealing with them. Some people can do this dirty work on their own, and some people might need help to do it. Therapy is a great place to acknowledge sources of pain and trauma. It is also a great place to learn how to deal with working through those issues for those that feel they need a little bit of help to do so. I was able to uncover, identify, and process some of my deepest, darkest traumas by doing the self-work in therapy. Being in a positive, supportive environment without judgement was a huge help in doing this. So if you think this approach might be helpful to you, find a therapist. Find a counselor. Find someone who can help you work through the pain and emotions. People in this profession are there for a reason, to HELP people. So if you need the help, seek it.

There will probably be a lot of emotions that you feel inside of you that are attached to these experiences that cause you hurt and pain. You might feel a great deal of resentment, guilt, shame, or even helplessness. It is so important to realize that these things happened, they are in the past, and they no longer have to have control over you and your life. They are powerless over you. We are not the abuse that happened to us. We are not the abandonment that we experienced. We do not identify as the things that others have maliciously called us. We are NOT what has happened to us. The sooner that we can accept and believe this idea, the sooner we can move past the pain and hurt in our lives to truly rise above them.

While we are still stuck in a place that we are allowing these things from our past to influence and control our inner peace and happiness, personal growth will be impossible. You will not be able to grow as a person if you don't disconnect yourself from these things and their control over your happiness. Your past is your past for a reason. It is behind you. It is gone. It is over. It is no longer here. We need to stop carrying it with us in a negative way.

I have gotten to a place where I can accept my past and the place it has brought me to. I am thankful for the experiences that shaped and molded me into the person I am today. I am grateful for some of the pain, hurt, and trauma I experienced in my past, because it taught me so many lessons that I carry with me moving forward in my life. I have been able to use my past to learn how to do things differently in my future. I have gained priceless knowledge that I will use moving forward in life to better myself and everything that I experience.

What can you learn from your pain and your hurt? What can you take away from the traumas you have experienced and use in a positive way moving forward? You can't erase the past and you can't change history. If we all had time machines, maybe there are some things we would go back and change if we could. But since that is not possible right now, we might as well try to use what we can from our past to learn and grow. We might as well turn pain into power. Life experiences are some of the greatest sources of knowledge and growth we will ever have available to us in our lives. They are absolutely priceless. We can use them to learn how to do things moving forward to better ourselves and our lives.

Never regret the things that once felt right or like they could have been the right things. I hate the word "regret" altogether to be honest. We should never regret anything because at one point in time it was probably what we thought we wanted or needed. Every little thing from your past that you may wish had never happened has contributed to exactly this spot you are in today. That's not necessarily a bad thing... It got you here. It got you looking to better your life. It got you to open this book. It got you wanting to reach a place of true inner happiness. It got you on the path to start creating your best life possible.

Look at the things you may have classified as "regrets" in your life. Look inward and identify the pain and hurt from you past that you carry within you. Identify the trauma from your past that has stayed with you for years and years. Let's identify it, accept it, and detach ourselves from it. Let's understand that we are not the things that have happened to us. We have so much more power over them than we ever knew we had, and it has always been there inside of us.

On our quest to do the hard work to find our innermost peace and happiness, what do we need to move passed for good? It's time to heal. It's time to patch up the spots of our hearts and souls that have been wounded over the years. It's time to stitch up the open wounds, and put band aids over the scrapes and scratches. It's time to truly heal inside. By healing inside, we can continue on in this journey to make each day of our lives a little bit better than the last one.

THINGS TO REMEMBER:

6 | THE COMPANY YOU KEEP

I firmly believe in all the girly, inspirational quotes you see on Instagram with black pretty lettering on bright white backgrounds about how "your vibe attracts your tribe" and "surround yourself with people like you"… This is such a powerful idea that is SO huge in creating your own true inner happiness. I just screenshot a quote the other day while scrolling through my Instagram feed because the Universe sent it in absolutely perfect timing with my writing this chapter. It read "surround yourself with people that reflect who you want to be and how you want to feel, energies are contagious." I couldn't have said it better my damn self! You catch the vibes of who and what you keep in your company, it's as simple as that. Energies of others are absolutely contagious! So, it is definitely time we start choosing wisely when it comes to who we keep close.

We're going to go over this idea again in the next chapter called The Purge in a very harsh, no-bullshit way, but we'll get more into the meaning and importance behind it first. Looking at the friends you keep in your circle is SO important. If you surround yourself with the most positive, encouraging, motivating tribe of people, they are bound to start rubbing off on you. You will soak up what they give off like a freakin' sponge. Believe it. Whether you yourself already share their go-getter, driven personality or you need a little boost in the motivation department, it's hard to be around people that inspire and motivate each other to grow and not start to gain a little bit of their positive vibes. That's a good thing! Soak it ALL in. If you keep company with people who are working hard to accomplish their goals and create their best life, odds are they are going to rub off on you. You will probably notice yourself starting to do some of the same things they do and thinking the ways they do. Please try to tell me you could be standing next to Tony Robbins or Oprah and not feel a little bit inspired in their presence. If you said you wouldn't... I'm calling bullshit.

I started to do this big time on social media. Rather than letting all the negative, drama-filled things a lot of people share on Facebook and Instagram clog up my feed, I started filling it with major positivity. I started to notice that every morning I reached for my phone once I was fully awake and would spend a few minutes mindlessly scrolling through Instagram before I even got out of my bed. Most of the time my feed was filled with lots of funny posts or just junk posts. Of course, I love seeing hilarious cat videos first thing on a Monday morning, but I decided I should fill this routine with a bit more purpose and positivity. So I started following more accounts that featured content about success. I followed a ton of female entrepreneur pages. I followed pages with spiritual messages. I followed motivational quote pages. I followed men and women who were out there showing the world what determination and hard work can do for you. My mindless morning Instagram scroll was now becoming an early morning pep talk for my mind via my Instagram account. Filling my morning with motivation, inspiration, and positivity filled my head with a brand new mindset to start every day with.

Something else I fell in love with that transformed my day first thing in the morning were several websites that deliver daily inspiration right to your phone or inbox. There are several I am currently subscribed to, my favorites being Shine texts, emails from the Universe, and The Newsette newsletter. Look these up and I promise you will want to incorporate them into your morning.

I have my Shine texts set to be delivered to my phone at 7:30 am every morning to wake me up. Each one has a link to a article about personal development with a cute little Instagram quote you can screenshot and share. Next I check my inbox for my email from the Universe, which usually has some sort of inspirational mantra you can start your day with. I literally check both of these before even getting out of bed. You probably see screenshots of them shared on my daily Instastory by 8:00 am if you follow me regularly. The Newsette newsletter is my newest discovery and addition to my morning routine. It is a newsletter featuring goals, interviews with inspirational, kick ass women, and some fashion and beauty mixed in too! I started making all of these a part of my routine and saw a huge positivity boost to my days.

Now when I woke up, I had that "here I come world, watch out!" attitude, which spilled into everything I did. Your mindset is everything when it comes to what you can do and accomplish in your life. It's time to start surrounding and infusing it with feel good vibes, positive affirmations, and people that have that like-minded positivity and drive that you want to feel in everything you do. You will notice that by starting the day by flooding your mind with things that inspire and motivate you, you will be more productive. You will get more shit done! You will absolutely OWN your morning.

Haven't you ever noticed how the people that live their lives with a positive outlook and inspirational attitude towards every day seem to be the ones that have all of the good things come to them like magnets? Sometimes, we wonder how these people seem to live a life where everything just seems easy naturally. Of course, the girl with the shining smile, optimistic attitude, and positive outlook has everything good going on in her life. Odds are it's not by luck or by chance, it's because she oozes the happiness and positivity she wants her life to be filled with, and that is what she attracts in return. It is her choice to create her day like this. It is her choice to be happy. It seems almost too simple and almost too good to be true, but I think it's a very basic attraction of energy that all of us have the capability of harnessing within our own skin and bones.

There are certain people in life that I know very well that I can honestly say it is almost humorous how often negative things are just attracted to them constantly. I mean it's not funny like I wish for bad things to come upon them, but its humorous to see in action just how much negative vibes and attitudes just start to attract more negativity tenfold. We all may know someone in our life just like this and know exactly what I'm talking about. They bitch and moan and complain about every little thing that doesn't go their way day in and day out. These kinds of people have a really hard time grasping the idea that sometimes things work out differently than you planned for a reason. These people certainly cannot grasp the idea that things go wrong so that other things can fall into place and go right instead. These people are your typical glass-half-empty, doomsday type of people every day of their lives. It's like a dark cloud just hangs over their head like you see in cartoons, trailing their every move. I don't know about you, but ain't nobody got time for that.

Obviously, sometimes there are just some people you cannot avoid at all times in your life. For example, there may be someone at work or someone in your family that is just a plain old Negative Nancy. I have some people like this in my family, which obviously I cannot just up and cut out from my life entirely. I've worked with a few people like this in the past, which I just tried to not acknowledge their pity party and keep going about my own work instead. I've had a few friends in the past that just always bitched about EVERYTHING. I simply try to limit my contact with people like this when it becomes negatively focused. I may try to rub off some of my optimism and good vibes on them in hopes it will lighten and brighten them up a little bit, but in the long run I find it best to leave a situation when it just becomes a breeding ground for negativity. Out of sight, out of mind.

If these negative people are a part of your life, and you have a choice of whether you include them in your everyday encounters, it might be time to start changing how much space and time they occupy in it. Don't think of limiting their time in a negative way, but rather that you are just infusing every day of your life with as much positivity, light, and happiness as humanly possible. You are just dodging a negativity bullet. You are consciously trying to up-level your daily experiences in your everyday life. There is nothing wrong with choosing people and situations that will only enhance that happiness and positivity when you have the ability to do so. You are simply keeping the best intentions for your life. You are intentionally letting in more of the positive and less of the negative.

I could no longer hang out around people whose only focus in life was partying. I lost all desire to dress up in hoochie outfits and stand by the bar all night. It literally just wanted to make me go home and do something I enjoyed instead the entire time I was there. I also realized that I could no longer relate to people that had no ambition or drive to excel in life. People who were complacent in their undesirable situations while they complained about them literally made me want to bounce my head off of a wall. I realized that the types of people I was keeping in my everyday life was shifting as I was making the changes necessary to better my life. They almost reflected each other simultaneously. I was choosing to surround myself with better people, and that just made me want to keep making my life better even more in any way that I could.

Now the company you keep can span into many different areas of your life. It's not only people that you interact with in person. There are a ton of incredible women out there on the internet that are just like you and I. I know it may seem weird to make friends on the internet. It may seem uncomfortable to some people to start a relationship or a friendship with someone you've never even seen face to face. But there's also an entire television show about people falling in love with people they have never met and being "catfished" on national television now… so does it really seem that far-fetched anymore? By the way, if you're looking for a little bit of entertainment, next time you have a minute to spare online google "Sarah Ordo Catfish"… Yes, that did happen. Yes, I did go through a period in life where I teased my hair like Amy Winehouse and wore headbands around it like a ninja. You're Welcome.

The first time I realized the power of the online community when it came to empowerment and motivation came in the form of a Facebook group. As you have picked up in my books and in various posts on my social media platforms, I am a huge fan of empowering, motivational, inspiring female authors and coaches. So when my favorite author and pseudo personal mentor Cara Alwill Leyba announced she was launching a Facebook group called The Slay Baby Collective that would feature a private group of only uplifting and positive female inspiration… You know I was clicking the 'Join Group' button on my laptop within 45 seconds of hearing it. If you enjoy this type of female-centered, feel good environment, you need to go join the group like yesterday. It is overflowing and bursting at the seams everyday with women who are all encouraging, supporting, and overflowing with positivity. It's like having thousands of girlfriends that only want the best for you at all times right on your smartphone or laptop. Honestly, I credit a huge portion of the success of my first self-published book to these ladies.

Not only were these ladies extremely supportive in my book launch, but they helped to promote it to others as well. They snapped screenshots of their books, left me glowing Amazon reviews, and sent personal messages praising my sharing my story. Being a member of this group led to my first two podcast interviews, a jewelry collab opportunity, and endless friendships with fellow entrepreneurs and authors. And while being a member of this online group gave me all of these amazing opportunities and connections, it's also just an amazing place to scroll through the posts when you're needing a little inspirational post to get your head back in the right place on an off day. Seriously, I am obsessed with the group and all of the amazing positivity it has brought into my life. I have since joined The Skinny Confidential group on Facebook as well, and it has a similar vibe for females everywhere can be a part of.

Staying with the theme of empowerment and inspiration, let's talk about the noise we surround ourselves with. I will be the first to admit that if you ever pass me on the freeway I will most likely be singing along to my '80s pop Pandora playing full blast… nine times out of ten it will be "Africa" by Toto just to help paint the mental picture for you a little bit more. But anyways, something I started doing was listening to more personal development focused audiobooks and podcasts for a portion of the time I was in my car from day to day. I also started to do this when I had my headphones in while running. Since I found it extremely difficult to make myself actually sit down for long periods of time to actually read, this became the next best option for me. It started rubbing off on me BIG time.

The biggest thing I noticed was that my motivation skyrocketed. You know those days where you feel so productive, so full of potential, and the ideas are just flowing out of you like water? That's how I feel after I listen to some good old inspirational noise. It really is like a total boost for me. I feel more positive, my mood is happier, and everything just seems a little bit better. Seriously, if I'm having an off morning or I feel like I've been slacking for a few days and not being my usual go-getter self, this is exactly what I do. I fill my ears up with something inspirational and uplifting. I listen to words that make me do a little more self-focusing. And I swear every time I do this, my day shifts. It can literally pull a 180 on my mood and give me the huge boost I need in the right direction. It's literally become something I now incorporate into my schedule on a daily basis because of the huge impact I've seen it have on my day.

If you know anything about the law of attraction, you know that the basic idea behind it is that what you put out, you attract. So if you are constantly sending out positivity and good vibes you will attract those same things back to you in return. So fill yourself up with as much positivity and happiness as you possibly can stand. Radiate good vibes as much as you can. Show love as much as you can. Show grace as much as you can. Show gratitude as much as you can. If you can attract a little bit more of each of these things into your life just by putting them out into the world yourself, why would you not? Just think of the power you have over what you will bring into your own life just by doing this. If sending out good things will bring more good things back to you, then SEND, SEND, and SEND some more!

Now on the contrary, if you send out bad vibes and negativity, you will attract those same not-so-desirable things back to you in return. It seems pretty basic and simple, right? I think the hardest part about following something like the law of attraction is to break old habits and make sure that you are continuously pumping out these positive vibes rather than negative ones. We all sometimes generate a little negativity out of a natural response or reflex and are not even aware of it. It's super easy to let something affect us negatively and really allow it to throw a wrench in our whole day if we let it. Remember how we mentioned earlier those negative people who always seem to attract more negative stuff into their life like magnets? The same idea can be directly related to the law of attraction. Put out bad, attract bad. And we do NOT want to attract any unnecessary bad here. No way, Jose.

Even if some not-so-desirable things are happening in your life, try to hold your focus on keeping things light and positive. It takes a bit of effort and intentionality to be able to look at the not so positive stuff and paint it in a more optimistic, "silver-lining" approach, no doubt about it. It takes a conscious effort to do what is not our typical response. But give it a try. If there is any truth behind the law of attraction, or if you believe it at all, then you might as well give it your best shot. Why would you not want to attract more good and positivity in your life if you could? I mean you did just buy a book about create your best life possible, right?

I began making changes about the people, things, and vibes I surrounded myself with in my own life before and during my second year of sobriety. I started to consciously look at the people and energies I was keeping company with. It became much easier with time to be able to identify the not so good people or things. I found that I was naturally being drawn to happier people, higher vibes, and more positive things. Bit by bit I began to naturally choose to spend time filling my days with positivity and happiness when I started to notice the amazing effects it had on my day to day life.

Even with simple changes like the ones I made in my morning Instagram routine, I was able to fill my days with more light and positivity. Starting out the day more positive made it easier to keep the rest of the day more positive. I'd like to try to explain to you how different and amazing it feels to approach each day as one that is happy and positive. Things are so much lighter. I am so much happier. Sometimes, I can't believe that things are as peaceful and positive in my life as they have been for a long time now. But I also realize that it is all because of ME. I made the changes and the intentional shifts and moves to turn my life into what it is today.

You have the absolute power to keep company with only the good things in your life. It is not selfish or wrong to only keep the best things and people around you. It is looking out for your own well-being. It is providing yourself what you need to up-level your life everyday. If you feel guilty at any point during this journey and this self-work, do not allow yourself to fall into that trap. It may feel foreign and different because IT IS foreign and different to you right now. But do you think the people with the most empowering, inspiring lives spend their time wondering if they are being selfish for giving themselves the things they need in life to be at that higher level? Not for one second.

While we have been focusing on how to keep company with only things that lift, inspire, and better you, we can also flip this to make this your responsibility to others too. Are you being the positivity and light in other people's lives? You can't preach all day about up-leveling your life if you are not showing the same to others in return.

Be someone's positivity source. While we are focusing so much on the self-work we are doing within our own selves, we need to be practicing what we preach too. Try to take notice in your interactions from day to day and see if you are being the positive light in someone else's day. Make sure that you too are reflecting the qualities of someone that you would want to keep company with in your own life. We don't want to be the hypocrite of the year over here while we are on our journey to bloom from the inside out.

I noticed myself doing this the most with my mother, which is super not okay. I know a lot of us have that relationship with someone like our mom. You obviously love and care for each other to the moon and back, but bickering about little things seems to just happen sometimes. I realized at times I would take my frustration out on her when I was dealing with things in other areas of my life that had me a bit on edge. I would slide a little attitude in my tone of voice or in my responses and almost started to feel guilty as I realized I was doing it. In this instance I was NOT being the company I would want to keep in my own life. Thankfully I'm able to catch myself doing it and kind of shut it off like 'what are you doing? Stop.'

You might be able to start catching yourself when you almost resort back to these ways, which is totally fine. Don't beat yourself up over it, it is not the end of the world. Just acknowledge it, own it, and work on it. You're not backtracking, you're simply changing. Change takes time. You're going to always be a work in progress when it comes to this kind of self-work. Things like this may seem like simple changes, but sometimes they take a little more effort to put in place constantly and make last. So give it time and let the changes become second nature naturally They say it takes 30 days to make a habit or a change that actually lasts, so cut yourself a little slack here.

Keep this practice up of always being aware of the company you keep and it will become almost automatic over time. Keep surrounding yourself with the things that promote inner happiness, peace, and blooming in every day of your life. Once you start to see the difference it can make in every single one of your days, you're going to want to do it forever. So surround yourself with as much positivity and light as humanly possible! Send out those positive vibes to the people around you as well! Up-level your day to day experiences to elevate your day to day life and you will begin to appreciate and enjoy each of them even more than the previous day. I'm addicted to this type of feeling... and soon you will be too.

THINGS TO REMEMBER:

_____

_____

_____

_____

_____

_____

_____

_____

_____

_____

_____

_____

_____

_____

_____

_____

_____

_____

_____

_____

7 | THE PURGE

When it comes to finding everything you need within you to reach true inner happiness, odds are you're probably going to find some things and/or people that you will realize are not for you anymore. A big hell no, a loud slamming door, and a big red "X" over the top of them. It's going to be hard. It's going to suck. Once you begin to look inward and do the self-work, you might start to realize that a lot of the things you thought were making you happy in life never really were. You may have thought that they were good all along, but when you start putting yourself and your well-being first, you may realize otherwise. The things you used to rely on for satisfaction might serve you no purpose anymore. The things that once brought you pleasure might not do that for you anymore. The way you used to live day to day just might not be the life you want anymore. You're probably going to find some things that are super negative and need to be pulled from your life like weeds in a garden of blooms. So what do you do at this point? You just might have to remove things. Welcome to The Purge.

Coming out of my first two years of sobriety, I can tell you that my life took a complete and total turn for the better in every way possible once I cut alcohol out of my life. Obviously, I purged my life of alcohol and drinking, but that purging also led to the getting rid of a lot of other things that no longer added to my new life in a positive way either. It wasn't easy to just start cutting things off left and right. Some things I could pinpoint right away that needed to change or go. Other things I wouldn't acknowledge right away, but over time they got the boot too. I'm not going to lie and say it was super easy. It was definitely easier said than done. There were people that I missed and things that I missed right away. I just had to keep reminding myself that I was making all these changes for a reason, to find true inner happiness and to create my best life. Refocusing and keeping my eye on the prize made it a little easier along the way.

When I saw the positive changes that started to happen in my life from simply removing alcohol from it, it only seemed natural to start looking at other things in my life and wondering what would happen if I removed other things as well. I was rebuilding my entire life one day at a time, so I began to start looking at all areas of it to improve it. It's not just about the people that are around you, it's about everything that you've been keeping around you. All aspects of the way you live your life can unknowingly affect you on the inside. I took a long, hard look inward and got pretty cut throat when it came to doing my own personal purging.

Things that I realized no longer were adding to my life in a positive way included friendships, relationships, habits, objects, thoughts, behaviors, etc. Anything that caused me to feel stress, negativity, anxiety, or pain got put on the chopping block. I'm going to keep it completely real with you and tell you that it was extremely hard to let go of some of these things. I held onto some of these things for a long time. I was holding onto them like an infant clings to their favorite blanky when their parents tries to ween them off of it.

The harsh reality and truth of it is that you're probably going to be removing a few things from your life if you want to truly look inward and find everything you need to be happy. You're going to need to be strong and do what's best for YOU. And removing some of these things just won't ever be easy. Period.

The things you cling to in an unhealthy way will most likely be the things that you need to remove the most. Especially when it comes to love and relationships, there are a lot of us that tend to hold onto the people that are the worst for us the longest. It's pretty twisted, but I think we can all name that one person we dated and stayed with for way too long, put up with way too much for, and don't really understand why when we look back at it. You may know someone that is doing this and is stuck in one of these relationships right now. I know that I personally know some young women that when I hear them talk about the horrible things their boyfriend has done while they are "kind of broken up"… I'm just sitting there like "…and why are you still with this guy again?" Sometimes it boggles my mind how people cling to unhealthy relationships for SO long without seeing what everyone else sees. It's like they lose all sense of their self-worth. But, we've all been there and we all know that love can be blinding to things that you would normally see when you are in the thick of it.

The biggest example I can think of when I relate to this idea of holding onto something in an unhealthy way was one of my relationships in my first year of sobriety. This relationship was manipulative and covered in lies. Cheating, abuse, you name it… this "relationship" had it. I'll be the first to admit now that I was being a f***ing idiot the entire time. If it had been someone else in my position, I would have been the friend telling them that they were a complete moron for staying.

For some odd reason, letting go of this particular person was absolutely horrible for me to do. It wrecked me emotionally down to the core. He wasn't even that amazing of a person, and he didn't really have much going for him at all in life at the time. Seriously, when I look back I'm just like… WHY? But regardless, sometimes the perfect cocktail of a newly sober girl with low self-worth who falls for an insecure professional manipulator can lead to that tornado of a destructive love story. These types of situations NEVER end with a "happily ever after" type scenario.

This just works to be an example of the types of people you might want to purge from your life. If you are single or casually dating, you might have some of these men or women in your life that you know aren't going to be good for you, but you simply keep them around out of familiarity and comfort. They are a quick fix when you're feeling lonely. They're a drunk text when you don't want to go home alone. Sorry to say it, but they are an external thing you just rely on or turn to when you are feeling lonely inside. We all have had them, and I'm just as guilty as you for keeping these people around way longer than they ever deserved to be there.

When I think back about those times in my own life, it makes me feel like I was being a little desperate to be completely honest. I felt the need to drag these men back into my life over and over again for what? For a confidence boost? For someone to be there for a hot minute? If there were reasons it didn't work out the first time, odds are some of those reasons are still there the second time around. And the third time around. So why continue to keep wasting our time and energy on these people?

You might be in a relationship that you know deep down isn't going to make it in the long run. Maybe you just haven't been ready to completely cut ties with this person just yet. That's fine, but you need to set a boundary line or an end point somewhere. If that line is crossed or the time has passed, it's time to let them go. You might like to fantasize about the idea that it might work out one day and not want to face the truth right away, but I think we all know that our gut is usually right most of the time when it comes to these things. As author Cara Alwill Leyba always reminds us followers of hers, "Trust your gut. That bitch knows what's up." Seriously, anytime I have ever gotten a weird feeling or a gut feeling like something was weird or just off, it was usually SPOT ON. Your intuition is usually more on point than you think.

If something about your relationship makes you feel bad about yourself, brings you down, or simply just doesn't feel easy, maybe it's not a positive thing for your life anymore. I know there's a million chick flicks that show us that love is hard and that you should totally endure anything and everything in life to fight for someone that you truly love. Sure, love takes work. Love takes compromise. Love takes sacrifice. But it's when love is no longer adding to your life in a positive way that you need to think about removing it. Nobody that truly loves you will ever intentionally hurt you or cause you harm. Bottom line. We're not talking about how to save a relationship here, we're focusing on what we need to remove to find your own true inner happiness. If you're looking to hear that you should put up with ANY bullshit because "I just love him"… well, then find another book, sister.

You will NEVER, at ANY point in your life need a man or a woman with you just to be okay. It's a beautiful thing when you find true love and someone that fits with the things you need in a romantic relationship in your life. But PLEASE, never be so desperate for a relationship that you sacrifice who you are or what you want or deserve just to be in one. I have done it and you have probably done it at some point before too. Guilty as charged. Well, guess what? We're not going to do that anymore. There are so many times I see girls doing this that I just want to shake them and yell 'Honey! What are you doing!?' Sometimes I think the younger girls of today have lost the idea of what a woman deserves in a relationship from someone else. I see girls get disrespected and treated like dirt over and over again, yet they keep coming back for more. We need to just stop dating assholes and f***boys. Period.

So right now you may be like 'Okay, we get it… get off of your soapbox girl,' but it is just a subject that really gets me talking. I was single for a very long time until I got into the relationship I am in now. And before that I was *that girl*. I was newly sober and absolutely lost at that time. I was that weak little girl letting myself be disrespected and treated terribly. I guess that is why I get so passionate about spreading that message, because I have been there. I have felt that type of hurt. No women (or man) ever deserves to be treated in a way that makes them feel that horrible. No individual deserves to be so intentionally hurt that they cry themselves to sleep for days. No women deserves to be depressed because a man told her she wasn't good enough. No man deserves to be disrespected because they were "too nice." Can we just stop being complete and total assholes to each other? Treat others the way you wish to be treated yourself.

Obviously, if you have a healthy, positive relationship already in your life you can ignore the last few parts of this chapter. Maybe keep it in your back pocket as a nice idea to reference back to if things ever change for you and your significant other. I hope and pray that this will not ever happen to you, but sometimes it does. Life throws a lot of twists and turns at us, and sometimes every relationship doesn't make it out alive. Sometimes situations and people change and they may get added onto the Purge List later on in life, but let's keep our fingers crossed for you and hope that doesn't happen.

Think about the people in your life that you call friends. Think about your gang, your tribe, and the people you surround yourself with. How do these people make you feel? Do they raise you up? Do they clap when you are successful at something? Are they there when you are crying in sweatpants with no makeup on? Who do you consider to be your BEST friends? The people you put on this list of who you consider to be your closest friends takes on new additions throughout our lives. We also may scratch off names from that same list many, many times over the years. Throughout our lives and the changes that happen in them, we are always meeting a ton of new people and letting go of some of the old ones along the way. This is totally normal. I would find it extremely odd if I ever met someone who had the exact same friends as an adult as they did throughout their entire childhood and young adult life. Unless you live in a town with a population of like 20 people. But even then, I feel like that would still be near impossible.

Letting go of unhealthy friendships can be really hard. I will tell you right off the bat that this one was a huge struggle for me. When you have become so used to spending time with a certain person or people, it can be super hard to let them go. Letting a friendship go can be harder than letting any boyfriend or girlfriend go. I've been there.

Someone I considered to be one of my best friends I haven't seen in well over a year now. For over half of that year I was desperately trying to keep that friendship alive when it should have already been gone long before that. For me to finally cut this one off completely it took a pretty big slap in the face. It took a Facebook status that was so blatantly and obviously making fun of something I shared on social media. I shared a Youtube video about my mental health journey during sobriety where I discussed my battles with depression and anxiety. It was a very personal subject and such a soft spot for me when I finally shared it publicly after keeping it hidden for quite some time. That was when I finally cut that one off. I laugh a little bit now that I immediately was like, "That's it. I'm unfriending her on EVERYTHING right now…" because that's what our generation does. Unfriending someone on social media is like the ultimate insult to us when in reality, who the f*** cares?

This person was no longer a friend to me. They were no longer there when I needed them. Now they were actually starting to cause me to feel actual hurt inside. So you know what I did? I removed them like they were a drag queen that lost while lip-syncing for their life on the latest episode of Ru Paul's Drag Race. And you know what? I no longer felt the need to reach out. I no longer felt the need to invite that friend to every girls' night or brunch. I no longer worried about that friend making the drunken mistakes I made in my past. I no longer felt shitty every time I tried making plans to hang out when they were "sick" yet posted snapchats wasted at the bar hours later. I finally decided I didn't need that kind of negativity in my life. Why? Because I had a ton of other amazing people in my life who DIDN'T make me feel that way.

Look at the people you spend your time with and think about how you feel inside when you are with them. It's time to prioritize the people that make you feel good. Spend more time with them. Build these friendships up and prioritize them over the friendships that don't run so deep. Remember, we are focusing on our own happiness above all else. We are working to find the things that make us feel happy inside, and that includes the people we are allowing to occupy any amount of our time in life. What we spend time doing and who we spend time doings those things with will directly influence our lives. Just as we went over in the previous chapter, its all about feeling positive and happiness with the relationships and friendships we keep. So who makes the cut in your life, and who doesn't?

What else can we possibly purge from our lives? Honestly you can pretty much purge anything you want. Just make sure you aren't hurting anyone else by doing so. You might cause a little bit of hurt feelings when you start to purge some of the people you need to cut from your life. Unfortunately it just might happen. But the people that you feel need to be removed from your life because they bring you negativity sometimes just need to be removed from it completely, and that's that. So you just have to do it and keep moving forward.

Do you need to remove certain things from your life that are making it hard for you to grow and move forward? Alcohol was the biggest thing I needed to purge. Hands down, no doubt about it. Addictions of any sort or level can cause a lot of pain and problems for not only yourself, but for everyone close to you in your life too. So alcohol was my first and biggest purge because I was able to easily identify that it was causing negative things to happen within my life. It brought chaos. It brought drama. It just brought a lot of negativity all around.

Do you need to purge something like alcohol or drugs from your own life? For a lot of people, it is possible to have a healthy relationship with alcohol, but for others that will never be the case. A good way to look at it is if your drinking (or using drugs, sex, gambling, etc.) is starting to have negative side effects on your life. Are these things starting to interfere with the way you live your life? Are these things causing problems between you and your family or friends? My negative relationship with alcohol caused problems within relationships with my family, it interfered with my friendships, and it contributed to an unhealthy lifestyle both physically and emotionally. It ultimately led to my almost losing my life, so clearly it was a big, fat, negative thing for me… it had to go.

The things that aren't serving you in a positive way can be draining. They can pull you down. They absolutely can be toxic to your life whether you already realized it or not. Some little things might not have as big of an impact on you, but some may be bringing you down on a daily basis in very drastic ways. Things can weigh very heavily on our subconscious and silently influence everything about the way we live our lives.

Look inward and decide what things you need to change or remove from your life. What do you need to take out of your life to find more inner peace and happiness? What would make you feel more content if it was removed from of your regular routine? What is holding you back or down?

Again, take baby steps. Don't delete all of your friends on Facebook, stop eating carbs altogether, or make any other rash decisions in your life… especially the carbs. But, really, just start looking at the things that don't leave you feeling fulfilled and happy. What just isn't doing it for you anymore? Is there a friendship where you strain to keep the relationship alive while the other person shows you little to no respect? Are you dating someone that puts their own well-being and happiness above yours? Are you going above and beyond for people that wouldn't do the same for you? Think about these things. Think about the people and things that continue to take from you, but do not give anything back that is positive in return.

When I started to purge my own life from the things that no longer made me feel good inside, it was A LOT. I did it slowly. One by one I acknowledged the things that I no longer needed to make myself feel content on the inside. The toxic friendship, the disrespectful men, the unhealthy habits… One by one I started to remove those things from my life. Some things that I removed were way more obvious than others, while other things I removed had a much bigger negative influence on me than I was even aware of. Once I started to remove one or two, it was easier to identify more things and remove them. Bettering my life by removing things from it became liberating, empowering, and almost exciting. At this point, I was really able to finally realize how much power I had over deciding what and who I let into my life. I had the power to purge anything from my life that I didn't need in it, and I was finally harnessing that power and using it.

And do you know what happened? I had less stress. I had less negativity. I had a new found sense of happiness inside of myself. It felt like a million pounds had been lifted off of my shoulders. I held my head a little bit higher. I began to be able to better identify things that would be positive for me to add into my life moving forward. I blocked the things that brought negativity into my life like the plague. I had such a newfound sense of clarity when it came to judging who and what were going to be good for me. This made it SO much easier. It didn't happen overnight, but with time it has just become a way of life. Now that I practice it regularly, there's no way in hell I plan on going back to the way it was before.

Once you start the self-work to better your life, you will just want to keep going on removing more negative things from it and adding more and more of the good, positive stuff. And you can never have too much good stuff. Once you feel this type of inner peace and happiness that comes with removing the bad and the negative, you won't ever want to give it up again. When you realize just how much power you have over making your life the best one possible, you will be limitless. It will become so much clearer to you what you need and what you do not need. I can promise you that once you master this area of knowing what you will and will not allow into your best life, you're never going to look back again.

THINGS TO REMEMBER:

8 | LOVE YOURSELF FIRST

Let's talk about self-love, because this is a big part of the foundation for finding everything we need within us to be happy! If we do not love ourselves then we have absolutely no chance of ever being able to find what we really need on the inside to feel content with life. So what is self-love? Well, Google defines self-love as the "regard for one's own well-being and happiness (chiefly considered as a desirable rather than narcissistic characteristic)." Let's take a moment to laugh at that little add on about self-love being desirable rather than being narcissistic. But we will get onto that topic in just a moment. So, basically, self-love is being aware and actively pursuing the things that will bring you well-being and happiness in your life. It seems simple enough, and many of you might be thinking "I'm already doing that." But are you, really? Are you really searching out the things that make YOU feel happy? Or are you simply searching out all of the things we have been told will make us feel happy?

Self-love is a funny thing to focus on. We do what we need to do on a daily basis to stay alive and get through the day. Of course we eat when we are hungry, we sleep when we are tired, and we drink when we are thirsty. But it's time to go way beyond these basic survival needs and find the things we can do to truly care for our minds, our bodies, and our souls. The kind of self-care I'm referring to is about treating yourself the way you'd want your ideal significant other in life treating you. Think about what sweet little gestures from another person make you feel happy, warm, and fuzzy inside. Is it a fresh bouquet of beautiful roses? Is it a home cooked meal at the end of a long day? Is it a pedicure when you've been working on your feet for long hours? Maybe it's a chick flick at home in your pajamas on a Friday night. Maybe it's an acknowledgement of your hard work during the week. Maybe it's a congratulations for all that you do. Maybe it is just being shown love for every inch of yourself, your body, and the life you've created.

Now onto the more important question... WHY CAN'T YOU DO THIS FOR YOUR DAMN SELF? Seriously, this is a 100% honest and blunt question. What in the world is stopping you from doing all of these things for yourself? Why would you allow someone else to give or do these things for you, yet you won't do them on your own? Do you deserve any of it any less if you don't have a significant other? HELL NO. You do not need someone else in your life to give you the things you deserve. It's time to start giving ourselves the things that make us feel loved to the deepest part of our hearts. Some of them may be actual objects or things, while others will be acts or behaviors. Self-love itself can be characterized by one of the words that make up the two word idea... SELF. We are every bit capable of doing these things on our own, just as the first word of the name suggests.

Let's jump back to that note about self-love being "desirable rather than narcissistic" really quickly. The fact that the definition itself feels the need to address that idea speaks for itself pretty loudly. Self-love can absolutely cross the line of being narcissistic. I'm sure anyone that has any life experience can think of someone they have met along the way that has crossed that line when it comes to loving themselves a little too much. People that prioritize their well-being and happiness at the cost of others are the ones that take self-love to an ugly, dark place. We do not wanna go there.

These types of narcissistic people are willing to do whatever they have to do, put down whoever they have to get past, and hurt whoever they need to along the way in order to make sure that they are the ones crossing the finish line first. This is not the self-love we want to exercise in our own lives. It is selfish, it is hurtful, and I bet it's going to bring those individuals that practice it a whole lot of bad karma one day down the line. I don't know about you, but I am a firm believer in karma and that what goes around comes around. I'm not trying to attract any bad karma into my life anytime soon!

If you have a significant other or are married, don't think that this chapter doesn't apply to you. Yes, I am looking at YOU too! Whether you have a partner that does or says these things for you or not, are you still doing them for yourself regardless? If your answer is no, then WHY NOT? If you have the sweetest man or woman in your life that treats you amazing with little surprises and gestures like these regularly, then BRAVO! You deserve that love in return that you give out so freely to others, and I'm so glad you have found someone that gives it back to you!

If you have someone that doesn't always do it 100% of the time, that's okay too. Everyone shows love in different ways, and some people just don't express theirs in the same way that others do. Some individuals show their love with words and loving statements. Others show their love with gifts. Others show their love with acts. There's no right or wrong way to show someone that you love them, but it is always a good thing to understand how your partner shows and receives love the best. If you would like more of these loving acts from your significant other, then talk to them about it and ask for them to practice it more often. Explain to them that you really feel appreciated when you are shown these simple little acts on a regular basis.

But, either way, there is still no reason for you to not be doing these things and showing yourself love DAILY whether you are single or not. Even if your boyfriend just made you a home-cooked dinner because you worked long hours, you can still run yourself that bubble bath too. Even if your husband surprised you with your favorite bouquet of flowers after a little fight that morning, you can still buy yourself your favorite bottle of wine to have a glass after dinner while watching the Housewives. There should never be a limit to have many acts of self-love and self-care that you can squeeze into any given day. Why? Because you deserve it, girl.

So how can we practice this thing we call self-love on a regular basis? Self love can be a million different things to a million different people. It can be materialistic, it can be mental, it can be emotional, it can be expensive, it can be free... it can be absolutely anything! The only protocol there is for determining what an act of self-love is, is that it has to be something that makes you feel good. It has to be something that makes you smile. It has to be something that you look forward to. It has to be all about your wants and your needs, honey!

Start to think about the things you enjoy in your everyday life. Think about the things you wish you could include in your everyday life more often. Maybe even make a list of things you consider to be self-love for yourself and refer back to it when an act is overdue. Do whatever you need to do to determine what some of the things are that you would classify into your own little category of self-love.

A lot of us are very busy with everyday life. Trust me, I get it. Some of you reading this may be working 60 hours a week at your job. Some of you may be a single parent holding your own little family together day to day. Some of you may travel constantly and live out of hotels. Some of you may just not feel like you have enough hours in the day ever. So when are you supposed to be able to drop everything and take yourself out for a 90 minute full body massage? I get it! I know you may be thinking you absolutely have zero time to fit in self-love acts on a daily basis. But, you are SO wrong.

You don't always need hours of free time to show yourself a little love. This idea is key! Finding realistic ways to make little self-love changes in your day to day routine is one of the easiest ways to start incorporating a little more love. It can be binge watching Game of Thrones for hours or it can be applying a face mask while you simultaneously bathe your 3 year old son in the bathtub. It takes about two seconds for us to take a look in the mirror and tell ourselves we look beautiful. Figure out what works for you and your lifestyle.

Some of us won't have time to devote hours to our own personal self-love activities. Some of us will struggle just to fit in five minutes of something for ourselves in our daily routine. I'm telling you, even if it is only those five little minutes... DO IT. Even if it is just those two seconds to tell ourselves we look beautiful. DO IT. No matter how many things are going on around you, no matter how much you have to get done, and no matter how silly it can seem. Start taking these moments to focus on YOU and what YOU need.

If you don't take the time to focus on yourself, who else will? Some of us might have someone that would, but for a lot of us, the answer might be nobody. This is why it is so crucial to make sure that you are paying attention to what you need to feel loved. Working on yourself and what you need is NEVER a waste of time. Time put into yourself is something that I see to be one of the most profitable and valuable things you can do in your daily life. Your mental health, your emotional health, and your well-being are only going to benefit from your showing yourself a little bit more of the love that you SO deserve.

Let's go over some examples of what self-love can look like on a daily basis, because it can be WAY more simple than you may be thinking. I'll use my own examples of ways that I fit my favorite, easy self-love acts into my daily routine to give you an idea of how easy it can be to fit them in without even trying very hard. Like most of us, I am all about simplicity, people!

Every morning when I wake up, I feed my Chihuahua, Kaya, take her outside, and I water my flowers and plants outside and/or inside. I absolutely love flowers! I buy myself flowers weekly and separate and arrange them into little vases around my place, and I also have them on my porch and little balcony. Seeing these blooms in the morning reminds me of their beauty and it instantly boosts my mood. It doesn't really take any extra time for this little daily reminder of self-love, I simply grab a bouquet at the market when I'm picking up groceries one day during the week. Succulents are also a personal favorite of mine because they are super easy not to kill (which I still somehow manage to do sometimes), and they last forever.

I love my coffee more than most other things in the morning, and many people can surely relate to this one as well. No matter how early I'm waking up or how stressed I am to get ready and rush out the door, I always make my morning coffee. I have a serious love for all the yummy, flavored creamers out there. My current stock in my fridge includes the coconut creme and salted caramel mocha flavors. If you haven't tried them, do yourself a favor and buy them. I ALWAYS make sure I have my yummy morning coffee as a little treat to get me going.

Depending on my schedule, my morning activities vary. Some mornings I will go for a quick run while listening to my favorite audio book through Audible (head over to www.audibletrial.com/sarahordo for a free 30-day trial). I have grown to absolutely love the morale boost I get from listening to self-development and self-help books. Podcasts are another soundtrack to my morning workouts on the regular. My faves includes the Style Your Mind Podcast with Cara Alwill Leyba, The Him & Her Podcast (from The Skinny Confidenntial) with Lauren Evarts & Michael Bostick, and The Fit Fierce Fabulous Podcast with Courtney Bentley. If I don't feel like thinking and really want to zone out, I'll turn on my favorite music instead. Being healthy makes me feel really good afterwards (I am miserable while running, though… don't let that fool you), so I consider it to be an act of self-care as well. I make sure to tell myself that I am a badass as I finish my workout too.

I always listen to music that makes me feel good while I get ready for the day. I have a serious love for '80s music currently, and as I've already name-dropped once, "Africa" by Toto is my go to favorite. For my morning shower, I use products in yummy scents of lavender, because I thoroughly enjoy the relaxing and soothing effects of lavender. Some days I will sit on the balcony and have coffee while I check my emails, and some days I will write a bit like I am right now. You bet your ass my feel good music is playing in the background and my coconut creme coffee is next to my laptop. It's a beautiful summer morning and I absolutely love being outside, so I have transferred all of my morning work outside for today instead of at my desk. I make sure to remind myself that I have worked so hard for all that I have and the place I am at in life.

If I am working elsewhere on that specific day, I will pack myself a lunch to look forward to enjoying. I try to keep my lunches healthy, nourishing, and full of things that make me feel good. If I am working at home for the day, I will grab some things from the fridge that I enjoy. Currently, that would include grape leaves, hummus, pita bread, and some fresh cherries from the market down the street. Eating well and eating things I enjoy makes me feel so satisfied, so I always have the things I enjoy on hand.

I will go about doing all of things I need to do during the day as I normally do. Whenever I am back home for the day, I will either make myself something yummy for dinner or have plans to meet up with friends or family for dinner. For example, last night after work I cooked up some chicken breast I cut into chunks with shawarma seasoning and I pan sautéed green beans in olive oil with a side of gnocchi in a little pasta sauce. Cooking for myself has become one of my biggest and favorite acts of self-love. Something about feeding my body and soul with the act really makes me feel taken care of and loved. I also thoroughly enjoy going out to eat and any of my friends can attest to that! I love sitting down for an amazing meal and relaxing while catching up with friends and laughing about whatever is going on in our lives. We had a girlfriends' dinner in downtown Detroit the other weekend at Andiamo by the water and let me tell you, it was so amazing to share a delicious meal by the water with people I enjoy.

As I wind down for the evening, I take off my makeup and throw my hair up in a knot. This is me in my natural and most favorite habitat! Although I do make-up for a living, something about taking it all off and being clean and fresh is so satisfying after a long day. I use my favorite skincare products and get into my comfiest pajamas. Call it my "pamper time" and maybe even call it excessive, but I tend to use at least five skincare products on my face most nights. Sometimes I will even do an "at home facial," using an at home peel or mask. Most days I try to convince my boyfriend to do a mask with me as well and document the entire thing on Instagram… Hey, I'm a girl and we enjoy this shit, okay?

At this point I may do a little work… Okay, to be completely honest, I have a terrible habit of always working at night on my laptop. It's a horrible habit and I am working on it! I try to make myself turn it off and unplug after a certain time, but I still struggle with it a bit. I usually watch something I enjoy on television or Netflix for a while before bed. I have a serious weakness for terrible yet addicting shows like *Teen Mom*, *My 600-lb Life*, any of the *Real Housewives* seasons, and any dating shows like *The Bachelor*. Sometimes I'll watch a movie instead. It just depends what I'm in the mood for that night.

When I decide to go to bed I take Kaya outside one last time and give her a nighttime treat, and then I make my way to brush my teeth. Before getting into bed, I turn on my bedside oil diffuser with my current favorite essential oils. My go to favorite right now is a combination of eucalyptus and lavender oils. I also turn on my Himalayan salt lamp because the warm glow is so soothing at bedtime. I always apply my favorite lip moisturizer and my hand and foot cream last thing before getting into the sheets. I cuddle up with Kaya in my bed, which I have draped with a beautiful white comforter and a white velvet blanket on top. I reflect on what I have been able to accomplish and what I am grateful for. I give myself kudos for a positive day. I talk to God for a few minutes thanking him for everything I have and then I drift off to sleep...

Do you see how many times I have snuck things into my daily schedule that are simple, tiny little acts and reminders of self-love? Some of them are things I don't even go out of my way to do at all, but rather little extras I can include in things I'm already doing. You don't need to make every act of love huge and outlandish, you can totally make them quick and simple things. This makes it much easier to fit them in. I hope that laying out a typical day of mine has shown you that you don't have to rearrange your day or set aside two hours for self-love. Some days, YES, I do that! But most days it is just a bunch of little, baby self-love acts and reminders that I sneak into my routine that make me feel good and elevate my day a bit.

Now stop and think about your day. How many times are there opportunities for you to sneak a little bit of self-love in there? Probably a lot more than you realize until you actually pay attention to it. That is my first challenge to you... to start making tiny changes in your everyday routine to incorporate more self-love. Just like I incorporate things that I love and enjoy into my routine on a daily basis, think about how you can do this too. Spend a little time outside, enjoy your morning coffee, enjoy a delicious meal, light a favorite candle or two… Give yourself as many little, effortless acts of self-love as you can in your daily life to automatically boost your happiness and elevate you day.

Once you start adding little acts of self-love, make a valid effort to focus on a few bigger acts of self-love each week. Maybe you will only be able to realistically set aside the time for one or two things, and that is fine! Something is better than nothing! Give yourself a little time block to do something that makes you feel good. Figure out what you can look forward to doing to treat yourself. Tell yourself what you need to hear. Whether it is a massage, a nap, a whole pizza, or just a reminder of how amazing you are, DO IT. You deserve it.

If you have a significant other or children, you could even think of ways to possibly include them in your self-love acts if you would like. Okay, some of you may be thinking that self-love means no spouse, no kids, no nothing! If that is the case, then go ahead and view it as your time for yourself. Chances are if you are raising a family you deserve a little time for yourself anyways! So go on and take it. But if you love spending time with your loved ones then go ahead and make them a part of the love too! This is just another perfect example of how you can make your definition of what self-love looks like into whatever works for you and your life.

There is no right or wrong way to show yourself a little love. Whatever fits into your mold of being considered self-love is your own little creation. So step one is going to be spreading the love. Spread the love so thick in your own little life that it becomes a part of everything you do. One of the biggest parts of finding out what we need to be happy and fulfilled on the inside is taking care of ourselves and our well-being. If we are not taking care of our minds, our bodies, and our souls, then we will never find a way to be truly happy by looking inward. These are the things that need to be the basis of our finding inner peace and happiness. Think of it as the foundation for our creating our best lives possible starting with our emotional and mental foundation we will be rebuilding from within.

Make sure that you are showing yourself regularly that you see and love the person that you are. Tell yourself "I see you girl." Give yourself a metaphorical hug and a pat on the back. Tell yourself how incredible you are. Show yourself all of the love you can.

What's wonderful about self-love is what happens when we start to love ourselves. I truly believe that until we love ourselves and are happy with ourselves, we will never be able to be in a happy, healthy relationship with anyone on the outside. We also won't be able to change our life into our best life if we are not able to show and feel love within ourselves comfortably. I know we have all seen the quotes of Pinterest with pretty pink lettering saying 'Love Yourself First'... and it's time we all started listening. Self-love is so crucial to our emotional well-being and in developing healthy relationships with others.

During my first year of sobriety, I was not showing myself any self-love. I was a mess. I was lost. I was just trying to rebuild my life and rediscover who I was. I definitely was not loving myself first at this point in my life, and it reflected on the way I lived that entire first year. I was not taking as good of care of myself, I was struggling to stand on my own two feet, and I was an emotional tornado.

When I was creating the title for *Sober as F****, I changed the subtitle of the book a few times. I knew I wanted to communicate the fact that the book was about my two year journey, but my two year journey of what? 'Rediscovery' was the first word that seemed to really fit into the subtitle because I felt that I had rediscovered who I was without alcohol for the first time in a long time. The second thing I chose to include in my subtitle was 'Self-Love' because that was what I learned to do again as I began to create my best life possible. If I didn't start loving myself and seeing my true self-worth, that journey would have never come full circle the way that it did. So the subtitle to the book became "My Two-Year Journey of Rediscovery & Self Love," and I couldn't have possibly thought of a better way to describe that long road I traveled on.

Self-love and learning to love yourself again in a whole and authentic way will give you the power to move mountains in your own life. Once you can love yourself completely, you will feel a whole new type of empowerment, strength, and beauty in everything that you do. Your confidence in yourself will skyrocket. You will be able to reach new levels in the things you are able to achieve. The shift that happens in your life when you begin showing yourself the love you have always deserved to receive is incredible. You will feel limitless. You will feel powerful. You will know how you deserve to be treated from others. It will elevate everything about the way you live your life moving forward. When it comes to creating inner happiness, self-love is a key piece of the puzzle, so let's give ourselves ALL the love.

THINGS TO REMEMBER:

_____

_____

_____

_____

_____

_____

_____

_____

_____

_____

_____

_____

_____

_____

_____

_____

9 | START DATING YOURSELF

This area is definitely the big one for me, and I have a feeling many people struggle with the idea of being alone. We are hardwired to be with others. We expect the "best day of your life" to be our wedding day. There are a million sappy love songs you could include on the soundtrack of your journey to find true love. There are hundreds of chick flicks and rom-coms on Netflix to paint every happily ever after scenario you could ever conjure up in your pretty little head. Love is all around us, and if you are single, you probably notice it even more. It seems like everyone is falling in love, getting married, and making babies.

Seriously, try having your own business where you do bridal hair and makeup every week. I spend the entire weekend watching women lace up their corset wedding dress and practice their self-written vows about how lucky they feel that they have met "The One." And then they would ask me "How are you single!?" It's no surprise that this is why we go through life looking for our soulmate.

Nobody wants to be alone. Well, some people do... but I'm

pretty sure they are in the minority a lot of the time. It is totally normal for us to want to find someone that can be our best friend and share our greatest moments in life with us. Who wouldn't want to be with someone who makes them feel loved all day everyday? Who wouldn't want to find their ultimate partner in crime? We are created to be social beings and have these types of connections with people. It is not healthy to be secluded and not interact with others in our daily lives. Don't get me wrong, I absolutely LOVE my alone time, but I also love being around people just as much (if not more). I don't know about you, but if I spend too much time at home without human face to face interaction (sorry, social media does NOT count!) I find myself feeling lonely and isolated.

Dating can be an absolute hot mess. Any of you reading this who are single and navigating the online dating world can probably attest to this. While some people meet great guys or girls online and live happily ever after, there are a whole lot of bad eggs out there as well. It is important to make sure that you don't lose sight of yourself, your morals, and what is important to you if you are actively dating. Sometimes, we are so desperate to just find someone, we will compromise these things just to be with someone else. HUGE MISTAKE. Doing this will eventually lead to you feeling resentful and like you have lost a part of yourself to another person. So why are we doing this? And why are we so desperate to be with someone else that we are willing to forget about ourselves and what we need along the way?

Ding, Ding, Ding! Once again, we are looking outward for someone else to make us happy on the inside. We can absolutely feel happiness as a result of being with someone else. Being with someone that brings out the best in you feels amazing and should be your ultimate goal when it comes to finding a significant other. Strive for this!

If you are going to be with someone, make sure that they make you want to be an even better version of you. Make sure they support you, encourage you, and add to the positivity in your life. Make sure that they support your process of innerblooming as you do the work to create your best life. Keep your happiness just as much in the forefront as you keep theirs. Make sure that there is a balance in your relationships, which in turn will keep them healthy and happy. When things are unbalanced, that is when we feel attached, anxious, and reliant on someone else to determine how we feel. This is not a healthy scenario when it comes to relationships.

You must always be careful to not lose part of yourself to a man (or woman). It is so easy to be blinded by only the good things in the honeymoon stage at the beginning of a relationship. We are absolutely crazy about this person and we want to spend as much time as possible with them. This is a beautiful feeling and can be such a happy time, so I'm not telling you to enjoy it any less. I am simply reminding you to make sure you don't give up your practice of self-love and prioritizing your well-being by focusing only on the other person. BALANCE. Before we will be able to find this type of balance, we need to find our own inner happiness first. By ourselves. It's the only way to stop relying on someone else to make us happy.

So when it comes to dating, I would like to suggest that you try something new. Try dating yourself for a change. You might be laughing now and saying "what the hell is she talking about?" but hear me out here! Why can't we date ourselves? When we date someone, we give (and receive) love, sweet words, thoughtful gestures, special gifts, little positive surprises, and so on, and so on. In order to date ourselves, we need to start doing things like this for ourselves. All I have to say is.. .WHY NOT? This idea borders the previous chapter all about self-love, because dating yourself is essentially going to involve actively practicing acts of self-love on a regular basis. After all, you can't seriously date someone you don't love... So we're going to need to be loving ourselves a LOT here. Practice treating yourself the way you would treat someone you are actively dating.

Now don't think that just because you are in a relationship or are married that nothing in this chapter can apply to you! The underlying idea of this entire "date yourself" message is to make sure you give yourself the things you need to feel good. It also directly relates to everything we just talked about while exploring the idea of self-love. Even though someone else might be already giving you all of the love and attention you crave, you can never receive too much of these things! There is no such thing as receiving too much love.

Do every sweet little thing you want to do to make your significant other happy, but don't stop doing the things for yourself that make you happy while you do so. The healthiest relationships are the ones where each person has their own identity, their own hobbies, and can spend time doing things away from their partner. It is so important to not lose sight of yourself and what you enjoy. It is very healthy to have your own life and your own time when you are sharing most of yours with someone else.

You can absolutely still be your own soulmate and date yourself even if you have already found your partner in crime in life. Think of it as a love affair of sorts with yourself. Whether you are married, dating, or single, I like to think that it is the only type of affair that is welcomed with open arms into any type of partnership dynamic. You're not looking to other places or to other people to add more love into your life, you're simply looking within yourself to make every day overflow with love just a little bit more. And there is never anything wrong with having just a little more love!

I have been guilty of looking for a man to make me feel complete inside for YEARS. It wouldn't be an hour from things ending with one guy before I would download all the dating apps again or reach out to old flames. Like so many women do, I was relying on men wanting me to make myself feel good. I was relying on attention from men to make me feel confident. I just kept thinking that once I met the right guy, that everything would just fall into place. Once I met someone that made me feel whole again I would be happy.

The most unhealthy idea that we can get stuck in our heads is that we NEED someone else in our lives showing us love to be happy. Of course, it's what we all want because who doesn't want to meet someone that makes us feel loved? Feeling loved and cared about is an indescribably amazing feeling when you are in the thick of it. No doubt about it. But the best thing we can do is to look inward to find the ability to show ourselves that kind of love as well.

Don't think you've got what you need within you to feel complete? Well you are absolutely dead wrong. We all have the capability of loving ourselves entirely deep down in our hearts. I don't care how many times you've screwed up. I don't care how many mistakes you have made. There is always a part of our hearts that holds everything we need to feel love again. It's a hard path to make it down sometimes and it is not one that ever truly ends.

I feel like I have gone through cycles in life when it comes to dating and being in relationships. There are times when I am completely content by myself, but then those times are followed by times where I would see others in relationships and wonder why I couldn't find someone to be with too. I struggled with this idea of dating myself for a long time, especially before and in the earliest stages of my sobriety. When I stopped drinking and partying, it just seemed like finding someone to occupy my time was the logical thing to do. I continued to meet men and go on dates thinking it would solve something for me, but it wasn't until I stopped looking for someone that I was able to truly bloom again. I had to get comfortable with myself again and start loving myself whether a man was in my life or not.

So where am I right now? Well, when I started writing this book I was actively dating myself. I know this sounds ridiculous and like something out of the most puffy, superficial, girl power podcast in the world, but let me explain... I was not cutting myself off from meeting people. I was not saying no to anyone that tried to ask me out or wanted to get to know me. I still went out on dates, absolutely. This girl deserves to get dressed up cute and be bought a nice dinner everyone once in a while (am I right, ladies!?). The mind frame I got myself into was that if someone wanted to pursue me or ask me out to dinner, then absolutely I would say yes. I had to cut out the men that were negative, draining, and only looking to get one thing out of our meeting. I was no longer wasting my time or energy on those that I didn't see contributing to my life in a positive way down the road.

I was no longer spending hours of my time searching for someone to make me feel happy inside. I stopped wasting my time aimlessly swiping through Tinder or Bumble when I got in bed at night. I was not chasing after anyone. I was letting whatever came to me, come to me. Simple as that. Because again, my main focus has been that if someone wants to come along and add to my life in a positive way then, hell yes, I would go out with them. But unless they were showing me that, well then, adios sir. I'll catch you up to where I am at now (at the time this book is released) later in this chapter, but for now let's dig deeper into how I began to focus on and date myself.

As ridiculous as it sounds, I enjoyed dating myself SO much. I thought it would be weird and awkward, but it was anything but that. And like I mentioned earlier about having a love affair with yourself even if you are in a serious relationship or married, you don't have to be single to do this. So how do you date yourself? You basically practice self-love and self-care to the fullest extent. We already went over a ton of examples of self-love and how to practice it, and you will definitely be applying those here. I'm basically just creating the most ideal, positive, enjoyable situations and life for myself everyday as much as possible.

Think about when you're dating someone. You typically fill up a good portion of your free time each week by planning on spending time together or doing things together. You both have Friday night free? Maybe you plan a little date night to your favorite Mexican place and to see that new movie you've both been wanting to see. He's off work early on Wednesday and you'll be home? You plan on cooking dinner for the both of you and falling asleep binge watching your favorite show on Netflix. Now PAUSE. Do this with yourself. I'm serious. Whether you have a significant other or not, why can't you plan a little date night with yourself where you have your favorite Mexican dish and see the movie you've been wanting to see? Give me one good reason. I'm waiting… Exactly. There is absolutely no good reason why you can't do these things for yourself whether you are single or taken.

I understand that there are some things we would do with someone else that some of us simply aren't comfortable doing alone. I'm still trying to master going out to dinner alone, so I totally feel you. If you aren't comfortable doing some of these things, just alter them to be more your style. Get a carryout from your favorite Mexican place if you aren't too keen on going out to eat alone. Or even cook it yourself. Rent the movie you want to see at home On Demand rather than going to the movies alone. Bottom line, do the things for yourself that you would do with someone else you are (or would be) dating. If it is something that makes you feel happy inside, than start doing it regardless. Because remember, inner happiness and well-being is our main goal here people.

Sometimes, while I'm practicing this dating myself thing I'd rather not be alone so much. I'm a total social butterfly, so I love to spend time with my girls. So while I'm dating *myself*, sometimes this includes planning a little girls' night too. Dating yourself does not necessarily mean you have to do whatever it is you want to do completely alone. Basically, I just turn my week into one that is filled with things I have planned for myself to fill my time with things I look forward to. So, yes, sometimes dating myself means reaching out to the girls and planning a little ladies steak dinner out or a bit of retail therapy at the mall. Because dating myself means that I give myself time to do things that make me feel good. I give myself an evening to look forward to with my girls that makes me feel happy. I am looking out for myself, taking care of myself, and doing things that make me enjoy life just as a significant other should.

Try dating yourself. Honestly, it's pretty simple if you really think about it. I lay out my weekly planner, look at my time for the week, and think about what I would enjoy or look forward to doing this week. What "dates" can I plan for myself during my week that will fill me up inside and make me feel full? Pedicure on your day off with a latte in hand? Pencil it in. Do I think I would enjoy going out to brunch and coffee with a friend on Sunday after church? I text a girlfriend, plan a time, and pencil it in. Do I want to enjoy homemade mac 'n cheese and watch that chick flick with Channing Tatum on Tuesday after a long day at work? Date night at home with myself. Pencil it in. That cute guy your friend introduced you to wants to take you out downtown on Saturday? If he seems like a nice guy, sure. Pencil it in.

See, it's not all about cutting people off when you say you are dating yourself. It's about creating special opportunities to do things with yourself that you would enjoy whether you are dating someone or not. It's about making each day a little more special for yourself. It's about putting your well-being and your happiness first. And do you know what is gonna happen? You're going to enjoy every day of your life a little bit more, day by day.

As I was practicing this act of dating myself while still being open to meeting others, it was an interesting road of finding a balance. It really jumped all over the place. There were times I was focusing way too much on meeting someone else. There were other times I totally hibernated and felt like I wasn't even trying to be open to the idea of meeting someone. There were times I was excited to get dressed up cute and be taken out. There were also times that something about a Netflix night in with my dog, a frozen pizza, and a big blanket was the way more attractive option after a long week. You've just got to find your balance because it's all about you and what you want and need at the time.

I do want to stress that if you are going to date others (or are already dating someone), it is SO important to identify what you deserve, what you want, and what you will allow into your life. Create some boundaries of what you will and will not accept from someone you are dating. If you are able to lay out and identify some guidelines for what you are willing to allow into your life, it will keep your mind focused on the self-work you are doing. We don't want to lose sight or get distracted by the guy telling you everything you want to hear and lose sight of our own self-work along the way. Don't get distracted by dating and allowing things, people, and habits back into your life that we are trying to get away from. Keep your focus.

When I started this book, I felt completely and totally at peace in my life. I was open to meeting someone and dating, but I was not chasing after it. I was not obsessing over it. I was not letting the idea that I haven't met someone yet bring me down inside or make me upset. I reassured myself repeatedly that everything happens in life exactly as it should and I was not missing out on anything. Things would fall into place when they were supposed to and not a minute sooner. I finally understood that where I was in life was exactly where I was meant to be, and if a man was meant to be a part of it then he would show up right on schedule. I have always really liked the quote that "What is for me will not pass me…" Seriously, if God or the Universe intend for you to meet a certain someone or be in a certain place in your life, they will surely make it happens. You can't control it or make it happen until it is supposed to happen. If it hasn't happened yet, then it just wasn't meant to be yet. Breathe easy, my child, and relax. It'll happen.

But, hell yes, I enjoyed putting myself first and being my own soulmate while I was dating myself for a long time. As silly as dating myself sounds when I say it out loud, not depriving myself of special things or "dates" always feels amazing. It is empowering. It is fulfilling. Try it and I promise you will see what I'm talking about!

If it seems weird and foreign to you, try it for just one night this week (or day depending on your schedule). Plan a little "me" night where you go out for, pick up, or cook something that sounds absolutely delicious to you. Make that pasta dish! Have that extra slice! This is your night. Watch that horrible chick flick for the 27th time in bed and cry even though you already know she ends up with Ryan Gosling. Rent that new movie you've been wanting to see but nobody wanted to go see with you. Binge the hell out of *13 Reasons*

Why on Netflix. Light all of your new seasonal Bath & Body Works candles. Eat the dark chocolate candies. Run the bubble bath. Create a whole little evening for yourself that sounds so amazing that you can actually feel yourself looking forward to it. Because first of all, you deserve it. And second of all, think of how good it makes you feel.

When I think about my little date nights with myself, I feel super excited about them now. I seriously look forward to them all day. I feel empowered and strong that I am able to give myself these kinds of special nights, whether I am single or not. And frankly, at this point, I don't think I'll ever be giving up my special little date nights with myself now that I have discovered how much I enjoy them. So my man is gonna just have to deal with that. Because this journey of mine is all about creating a life for myself that puts my happiness and my inner peace first. I plan to keep on looking deep within myself to find out what I need to do in my own life to make sure that I am content and fulfilled on the inside. I am creating my life as one that fills me up inside and makes me completely content whether I am with someone else or not. So, in the future, he can just go to his man cave while I take a bubble bath and listen to Beyonce before watching *The Notebook* for a 28th time.

So I suppose I should add that while I was deep in the middle of dating myself, I met someone truly wonderful. When I focused more on bettering myself, we found each other. I continued to act in the same ways as if I was dating myself even though I began dating someone new. And guess what? We are starting to share our lives together. And I'm still dating myself, too. I do every little thing to make our relationship amazing and special, but I also keep doing all of the little things for myself that I enjoyed before we met. I am loving myself as much as I am loving him.

I can honestly say that I have never been in a healthier place when it comes to being in a relationship. I can also honestly tell you 200% that once you can date and love yourself on the inside, you can have the best love of your life on the outside. I'm my own living proof of that right now, and I couldn't be happier. Not only am I blooming from the inside and living my best life possible, but I'm now experiencing my best love possible, too.

THINGS TO REMEMBER:

_____

_____

_____

_____

_____

_____

_____

_____

_____

_____

_____

_____

_____

_____

_____

_____

_____

_____

10 | SOUL FOOD

When something soothes and truly fulfills the mind, body, and soul you will feel it. Think of these things as the "soul food" that we need to feel full and nourished in our lives. Soul food can take many, many forms for different people. I like to think of soul food as anything that makes me feel fulfilled, inspired, and full of love. Kind of like my mama's homemade baked mac 'n cheese, with even the sauce made from scratch… Full of carbs, cheesy goodness, and love. During my early sobriety I had to find a lot of things to take the place of alcohol and the many hours I had once spent partying and in a drunken haze. These things had to be positive and healthy things I could use to not only fill my time, but also to better myself. They had to be things that added to my life in positive way. They had to be things that raised my spirits and helped me enjoy everyday of my new sober life. They had to be things that supported my continued blooming from the inside. These things have now become the "soul food" I include in my daily life to make my heart feel happy and full.

Figuring out what your "soul food" is can be quite an enjoyable experience. You're going to expose yourself to any and every thing that makes you happy and is a positive influence on you emotionally, mentally, and physically. It's like you're giving yourself all the feel-good things that fill you up all day, every day (and who wouldn't want that!?). Start testing out all kinds of new and different things to see what really hits home for you. There are no rules for finding out what your "soul food" is except for that is has to be positive, healthy things that makes you feel good inside and feeds your soul. It should be comforting. It should make you feel warm, fuzzy, and at home within yourself. No matter what is going on outside yourself, these things should be able to bring you peace, comfort, and a whole lotta feel-good vibes on the inside.

Right now I am in the full throws of practicing what I preach. Figuring out what all of my "soul food" things are has been the shit… I'm making myself amazing meals. I'm catching up on a ton of movies as I'm spending more nights in relaxing. I'm overloading myself with a ton of motivational and inspirational podcasts and books. I'm enjoying time with friends. I'm going to church. I'm booking trips. I'm exploring any and every avenue of things that make me feel good inside and fill me up. I'm putting myself FIRST and I'm feeding both my heart and my soul daily.

My only concern right now is figuring out what things will further enhance my life and how I feel on the inside. I'm finding all of the things that contribute to my innerblooming. Sometimes it makes me feel like the most selfish, narcissistic person EVER. You may feel the same if you have never lived this way before either. But let's snap out of it and realize that there is absolutely nothing wrong with focusing on yourself. There is nothing wrong with focusing on what you need to do or fill yourself up with to have the biggest, best life possible. Now back to the self-work. What truly feeds your soul?

Take a trip. Cook yourself a nourishing dinner. Take up a yoga class. Listen to a motivational podcast. Buy a new self-help book. Join online motivational Facebook groups. Go to bed early. Join a church. Cuddle with your furbaby. Grab lunch with friends. Spend all day in your pajamas. Literally any of these things can be your own kind of "soul food". But these are just a few examples of what could possibly be the things that make you feel good inside and feed your soul. There could be a million possibilities for a million different people of what fits their idea of what nourishes their own mind, body, and soul. So dive in and start exploring what yours could be! Remember that there are no rules except for that it must be a positive thing that make you feel comfortable, fulfilled, inspired, and nourished inside.

When I find things that are my TRUE "soul food" they tend to make me feel like I could overflow with emotion. Sometimes it feels like my heart is a balloon filling up with happiness so big that it could pop and burst open into pieces at any minute. I often feel like I am just spilling happiness out of my heart inside my entire body. The feeling can be almost indescribable at times when you find something that fully feeds and nourishes your entire soul. You feel so satisfied and so full of life that it can be hard to explain the feeling to someone that has never felt it before. If you have read my previous books, you have probably heard me describe traveling as something that makes me feel "high on life" at times. I feel so full and content when I am in nature and in new places in the world. I feel full to the brim with richness and I am completely satisfied.

So one of my biggest "soul food" discoveries so far has definitely been traveling. I plan trips and give myself time off occasionally throughout the year to give myself the opportunity to treat myself to new places and new experiences. When I go on these trips, I often went alone up until recently. Solo traveling can be a little scary and awkward at first, but it has proven to be one of the most fulfilling and empowering forms of "soul food" in my own life.

Traveling alone forced me to learn to be comfortable by myself for long periods of time, which is something I had always struggled with. It forced me to do a lot of self-reflection and focus on myself and my emotions when I spent so much time alone. This has been the most valuable thing I have discovered along my journey in sobriety. Learning to be comfortable alone and to actually enjoy my alone time has been a process, but so rewarding for my inner-self. It was a challenge that really forced my soul to grow and really take in more and more with each trip that I went on. I am now healthier emotionally and mentally, and I have a newfound sense of self-confidence and stability inside of me knowing that I can go see amazing places completely on my own and enjoy it.

Today as I am working on this chapter again, I am up in Northern Michigan at my family's cottage on the lake. If you have read my fist book, you may already be a little bit familiar with this place. I have been coming up here since I was a baby, but as an adult this place has come to hold so much more meaning to me. Being here is definitely another form of "soul food" for me. This place holds a lot of nostalgia and childhood memories of my growing up spending my summers here. We ran through huge piles of leaves, caught buckets full of frogs, swam in Lake Huron, ate grilled cheese on the picnic bench by the water, and swung on tree swings while swatting away the black flies. This place is calm. This place is simple. This place is beautiful. This place feels like a simpler time. This place feels like home.

Coming here as an adult I appreciate the beauty of it a little bit more. I try to visit for several days at a time at least a few times every summer. I sit outside and watch the sunset over the water. I have my morning coffee by the lake while writing on my laptop. I watch my Chihuahua, Kaya, run through the acre of land and lay in the sunny grass, totally loving her life. This place feeds my heart and my soul. The absolute simplicity and beauty of the lake here fills me up inside. The fact that I barely have cell phone service and can't waste time texting or on social media forces me to stop working and relax, and that is surprisingly refreshing as well. Sitting here watching the sunset with a cool evening breeze coming in and hearing birds chatter... I love taking it all in.

Another source of "soul food" for me is cooking, and of course, eating. Because really, who doesn't love to eat!? Plus, we are talking about FEEDING our souls, right? My relationship with food changed when I started looking at what I put into my body as a form of nourishment. Feeling good on the inside starts with how we are taking care of our bodies, and what we put into them plays a huge role in this. As I've stated previously, I don't deprive myself of any type of food that I truly enjoy, but I do practice moderation. I will absolutely devour several slices of hot, delicious pizza if I'm craving it. No doubt about it. I will also kill a mac 'n cheese cheeseburger at the Rusted Crow in Detroit (Sorry, not sorry). I don't deprive myself of any of the things I enjoy eating, but I do try to keep it under control most of the time. Honestly, I actually feel better when I eat better. Too many fries, pizzas, and burgers will eventually lead me to feel a little bit shitty physically.

One of my favorite "soul food" acts is definitely making myself a home cooked meal. Something about the act of buying fresh ingredients, turning on some music, lighting candles, and preparing myself a meal fills up my heart and soul. It's my absolute favorite way to practice self-love and self-care. It is also my favorite way to have a "date night" with myself. I find the entire act in itself to be so fulfilling in more than just a physical way. By preparing myself dinner I am feeding my hunger, nourishing my body, and comforting my soul. Talk about the ultimate way to fill yourself up in more ways than one. This is why you will find me posting photos of meals I've prepared all over my Instagram account. I love preparing amazing meals for myself and making myself feel truly nourished inside and out. And since this girl LOVES to eat, obviously that helps too.

I am one of the biggest fans of motivational books, podcasts, Facebook groups, Instagram pages, and so on and so on. Yes, I am one of those girls that posts a shit ton of pretty, motivational quotes all over my social media. There is a good chance you may have even heard about my books in one of these groups online. The girl gangs I joined and the support these women have shown me fills me up so much with love! The main idea for this area of "soul food" in my life is that I have chosen to incorporate positivity driven, personal development into my daily life. So I surround myself with words that lift me up, stories that inspire me, and people that make my heart feel full. Finding what we need within us to feel happy, confident, and growing as a person depends a lot on our mood, and our mood depends a lot on what we are surrounding ourselves with. So, surround yourself with as much positivity to feed your heart and soul as possible! I find that when I include more of these books, podcasts, blog posts, etc. into my daily life that the motivation feeds my soul. It makes me so full of life and hungry for more. I feel inspired in all of my dreams. I feel supported and comfortable in my ventures when I hear the words of others who have done similar things.

I love feeding myself some "soul food" by listening to motivational podcasts and audiobooks regularly. I love a good old book to hold and read in my hands, but with my busy, entrepreneur lifestyle having me always on the go, I don't always have the time to sit and read. Popping some earbuds in and having a ton of inspirational, mood-boosting words at your convenience at all times is amazing. I try to listen to one of these podcasts or books when I am driving in the car as often as I can. If I've got a thirty minute drive to a client ahead of myself, I might as well fit in something beneficial and inspiring that feeds my soul while I have the chance to do so.

It's hard to not feel good deep down inside when you are listening to the words of people who encourage and motivate thousands of people daily. I find that even when I'm in a funk or start my day off on the wrong foot, I can always throw on a podcast or audiobook and let the words do a little work to feed my heart and soul what they crave. Seriously, try it the next time you feel like you just need a little bit of comfort and nourishment inside. Audiobooks are definitely the most effective form of this type of "soul food" for me. Something about being read a story just feels calming and soothing, possibly because it puts us into a role similar of being told a story like we were when we were a child. You already know I love Cara Alwill Leyba's books... and anything from writers like Gabrielle Bernstein, Rebecca Campbell, Sheila Niequist, and Jen Sincero. But I am CONSTANTLY finding new audiobooks for a little extra "soul food" and positivity in my days!

Let's be honest…I've never been one of those girls that wakes up and looks forward to that morning workout. For years I have forced myself to work out at least twice a week to maintain a normal weight. I love eating so it has just been necessary. As I got sober, my views on taking care of my body changed drastically. I started to take a lot more pride in caring for my body.

I had trashed myself physically for years with drugs and alcohol, and I wanted to actually start caring for myself physically. It's taken a little experimentation, but in time I have been able to turn physical activity into "soul food." It could just be the rush of endorphins, but I have grown to enjoy morning runs with good music or an audiobook in the background. It's like combining personal development with something that is good for you physically. It raises my confidence. It makes me feel strong. It makes me feel healthy. It just makes me feel good inside now. And as an added side benefit, it's like free therapy. I can totally zone out and clear my head while I'm on a long run. It's become an amazing way to knock out stress. Taking care of my body is something I view now as nourishing and fulfilling. Keeping my body strength and healthy is an all new form of "soul food" for me.

So, I've never been a total yoga girl. I totally double click and like all of the awesome yoga videos I see the women I follow post on social media, but for some reason yoga never appealed to me in the past. I was more of a hardcore runner and weights type of girl. If I was going to work out, I wanted to FEEL it. But low and behold, I am starting to get turned on to yoga. Now I realize why so many people are obsessed with it, and I have a feeling it's about to be one of my new favorite types of "soul food" moving forward.

I looked up an "Easy Yoga Flow" on YouTube the other day after my usual run and workout. Something just kept sparking my interest to try it out. First of all, I had to stop for a minute halfway through because my arms were hurting so much. Holy shit, I had NO idea how hard yoga can be! I thought I wouldn't feel like I was getting a good enough workout by just doing yoga, and here I was unable to even complete a 12-minute flow without giving my arms a break! But besides the physical aspect of it, I was shocked at how relaxed and calm I felt. I felt good. Really good. And that was how I discovered that I needed to get into yoga immediately.

So I'm a little late to the game, obviously, but I'm so stoked to introduce yoga as a new item on my "soul food" menu. It's gonna take a little time and practice to get better at it and get stronger, but it is so fulfilling! Not only does it strengthen and keep your body feeling amazing, but it does wonders to ease your mind while feeding and nourishing your soul. You get to block out everything, be one with your own thoughts, and truly relax. Pair it with some soothing background music and essential oils, and it's like you're in a spa and therapy session all rolled into one. Yoga can relax your body, ease your mind, clear your thoughts, and nourish your mental state. Seriously, what took me so long to discover it? It's another form of the ultimate "soul food." I've never been able to get into meditation because I hate sitting still. Yoga has now come to be my solution to that problem. Yoga is like meditation without sitting still, and that is a whole lot easier for this busy body to actually do.

So there is an area of what I consider to be "soul food" in my life that a lot of different people include in their own, but it is a touchy subject and can go in many different directions. I am talking about religion, spirituality, or whatever type of belief or connection to a higher power or the Universe you might have. There are no right or wrong beliefs when it comes to this area. It is so dependent on your individual beliefs and whether you choose to embrace one of these ideas or not. But I can personally say that believing in something bigger than yourself can be a very life-changing and powerful experience.

I was raised Catholic and attended a private Catholic school throughout my childhood. Clearly, I had strayed from any type of religion for quite some time. Upon nearing my one-year anniversary of sobriety, I joined a non-denominational church because I was so lost that I was desperate for somewhere to find some guidance and support. If religion or church is not your thing, this probably won't relate to you, but once I opened myself up to believing again a lot of things in my life got much more clear to me. I shared in *Sober as F**** in detail all of the crazy symbolic dreams I began to have and strange signs I would see in my life. I also became very aware of my spirituality and the idea of the Universe having power to influence and give us what we need in our lives. Becoming more connected with my spirit and energy, things got lighter. Knowing that there is something out there much greater than me was so interesting. I felt like things started to come into and get pulled from my life more and more each time I looked for some sort of spiritual guidance.

I can 100% say with complete confidence that once I reconnected with God and the higher powers of the Universe, things just started to feel more right. Things started to be shown to me when I asked for answers. My life began to change. I felt that I could trust in the timing of my life and the things that were happening in it. Having faith in something bigger than yourself can do wonders for you inside. My heart felt like it would bloom from the inside with overwhelming power and beauty while I was at church. Hearing stories from the Bible interpreted into everyday situations gave me such guidance. While I may not agree with every single thing taught in church, I take what ideas and lessons I can and I apply them to my own life. I take what I need to better my life and grow as a person spiritually.

Even if you are unsure about where you fall when it comes to religion, spirituality, or higher powers, try exploring the idea a bit. I couldn't believe how much having faith in someone or something bigger than myself has offered me a more connected life with the world. Things felt right and everything seemed like it was moving towards a sort of bigger purpose. Having faith in something and praying or meditating with it is such a massive form of nourishing the soul. If you are a religious person, you know what I'm talking about. There have been many times in church I have felt goosebumps all over my skin while singing to God. I have felt my eyes fill with tears when the message of the day's passage relates directly to what I really needed to hear on that day. I have such strong beliefs that this practice and area of my life is something that feeds my heart and soul like not much else can.

And how could I forget... WRITING. I never knew how much writing could feed my heart and soul until I jumped head first into it. Writing my earliest blog posts and writing my first book quelled a hunger that I didn't know I even had inside. It filled up a part of me that I didn't even know was there. Being able to inspire and help others by doing so has made it even more fulfilling. I always saw a lot of people writing and journaling in their free time but it never clicked with me why they enjoyed it so much. Now I TOTALLY get it.

I could go on and on and on about what all of my "soul food" things are, but you get the idea. I can honestly say that paying attention to the things that I feel feed what I crave and nourish me inside has been a total game changer. When we put this kind of focus and attention on what can fill up our hearts and our souls we have SO much power to just continue bettering ourselves. You will grow emotionally. You will feel more balanced. You will feel more content. All I can say is, the more of these things you allow to fill you up and make you feel taken care of and fulfilled, the better.

You know exactly the feelings I'm talking about here. Those feel-good feelings. Those feelings you get when you spend time at your mama's house. How you feel when you're with that childhood friend you could tell anything to. How your heart feels when you're listening to your favorite song, the one you love so much it gives you goosebumps when you hear it. It feels like a warm hug. It feels like a kiss on the forehead as you are falling asleep. It's like the reassuring words from someone that you look up to. It's like that homemade mac n' cheese you craved as a child. You get the picture.

So identify your "soul food" and practice it often. Practice it every day if you want to. If you're not sure where to start, feel free to use some of my examples to start exploring different options of what yours might be. You'll know when you find something that works for you. Your heart will feel full and your soul will feel nourished. You will feel that type of indescribable, inspiring rush of emotions all throughout your body. You may get a little emotional, and that's fine. We are growing so much on the inside as we go through this process of innerblooming, and it can definitely be something that triggers a lot of emotion. Our lives are turning into something more beautiful on both the inside and outside than we ever knew was even possible.

When you feel this rush of feelings and emotions inside, take notice of how things start to change in your everyday life. The more you feed your heart and soul with good things, the more happiness and positive vibes you will see spilling into everything you do. Every day will seem a little bit happier. Every day will be a little bit brighter. You will be even more inspired. You will feel more fulfilled on the inside. You are going to grow and bloom so much in your heart and your soul along the way. Things will just be on the up and up in all areas of your inner peace and well-being, I promise. So feed yourself up until your heart and soul feel more full and nourished than ever before, and definitely go back for seconds!

THINGS TO REMEMBER:

11 | MAKE EVERY DAY SPECIAL

Things get repetitive. Day after day, we may be following the exact same routine… Get up, coffee, shower, work, eat, sleep. Wake up. Do it again. I mean, just typing that out like that dropped my happiness level at least three points. Things get repetitive if we let them. Days melt into each other if we allow them to. Things get complacent if we are never looking for something new or more. When the laundry list of things you have to do can seem never-ending, we tend to make the actions of our days like the literal crossing off of a massive to do list we have created for ourselves. We slip into a routine, we lack livelihood in our days, and we become robots following the same old, same old every day. There is no room for excitement. There is no room for spontaneity. There is no room for anything to shake things up. I don't know about you, but the thought of doing the same thing every day, playing it safe, and always sticking to the plan sounds just plain old BORING. Cue the snoring here.

This whole chapter actually got sparked from a conversation I had with my boyfriend the other evening. (Side note, I jump around when I am writing. So if you're confused when I say I'm single in one chapter and have a boyfriend in another, my jumping around while writing for months is why.) We had just finished having a beautiful little Wednesday evening dinner on the balcony of my townhouse. I made baked parmesan chicken breasts, caesar salad, and spinach fettuccine pasta with spinach and zucchini marinara sauce (yes, this girl can seriously cook). *insert hair flip emoji here*

We originally had other plans that got switched last minute, but I ran to the market down the street to grab things to cook and made this beautiful little meal instead. We decided to eat outside on the balcony because it was a beautiful August evening in Michigan. Talk about your perfect little impromptu dinner together at home, right?

We even ended the night by taking my Chihuahua, Kaya, for a walk around the little lake here on the property. This quickly led to the decision that we should totally drive to Wyandotte, the next town over by the water, and get frozen yogurt with heaping piles of as many cheesecake pieces, brownie bites, cookie dough chunks, hot fudge, strawberries, and Kit-Kats that we could possibly fit into our bowls. This led to my suggestion that we go for a little drive on the island Grosse Ile and look at the big houses while listening to and singing along with country music playing (seriously… could we be any more disgustingly couple-y?).

But back to the conversation that started this whole evening. My boyfriend and I were having one of our typical 200% honest, deep conversations. This is one thing I love about our relationship so far is our ability to be completely open to talking about absolutely ANYTHING without holding back. But that's a whole other book I could write (wink, wink). He had brought up the topic of wondering if I would ever get "bored" with our lives being just everyday normal lives like this, cancelling plans to just have dinner at home instead.

Let me rewind a little first. We met on a Sunday evening and he was buying a plane ticket to go on a trip to coastal Maine with me (that I already had booked) by Tuesday afternoon just three days after meeting me in person. We literally began our relationship and fell in love in one of the most beautiful places that held such a special place to me in my heart within a week of knowing each other.

It was one of the best weeks of my life, it was absolutely surreal, and every second of it was absolutely perfect. You can see how our love story started out feeling like something from a movie or fairy tale. So yes, coming home to actually start normal lives together was very different from how we started. We very well could have become "bored" with things since they wouldn't be anything like all of the perfect lobster dinners on the ocean we shared and the cuddly nights spent in a tiny little cabin by the woods.

When he asked about if I would ever get bored with these "normal" days and nights, I immediately went into preaching mode. As I spoke about the topic out loud, I realized this amazing practice that I had already been doing throughout my sobriety that I never really identified as I was doing it.

Since getting sober, one way I have focused on promoting happiness and positivity in my life is to give myself little things to look forward to. I consciously tried to take one thing about every day and make it a little bit more special. I tried to make every day more meaningful. By giving myself one little special thing (or sometimes multiple things) to look forward to every day, I became more happy. That one thing in my day became something that I focused on and waited for. As silly as it may sound, those little things were holding me together in a time where I felt like I was completely falling apart and struggling to keep it all together.

Even if I had the most typical, regular day, hyping myself up for the idea that I was going to go home and take a bubble bath with candles lit and music playing softly in the background gave me something to be excited about. Little things like getting a pedicure while I was already going to the nail salon to get my nails done, provided a tiny upgrade to my regular errands and routine. Setting aside time to have my morning coffee and write made a regular morning more satisfying. I was elevating my daily experiences, upgrading my lifestyle, and making something special about each and every single day because it made them more meaningful and it made me happier.

As I preached this idea to him, I realized how truly important this had been to my finding true and authentic happiness within myself. Upgrading the regular things about my life allowed me to appreciate it even more. It made me bloom from the inside with gratitude. I had already been practicing this idea for months in an attempt to practice self-love and date myself on a daily basis.

I realized that this same idea of making something special about everyday could also be applied to my relationships as well. It can really be applied to any part of your life... family, career, friends, anything. If you let things become repetitive, normal, and routine over and over again, they begin to lack excitement and that spark we yearn for. We simply go through the motions and can start to lose our passion and our spark for these things that we may have once had. By infusing these everyday situations and experiences with something to make them more special, no matter how big or small, it shifts the way we look at and feel about all of these things. It can make something ordinary into something far more extraordinary than it may have otherwise been.

Sure, we could have let our change of plans lead to a Styrofoam-boxed, carryout dinner last minute. We could have been bummed by our change of plans and just given up on having a special night altogether. But as I have now explained, I LOVE making something special about every day. Something that I look forward to and get excited about. So instead of letting the evening go to shit and be nothing special at all, I made it into something new spontaneously. I cooked our amazing dinner, which made it feel a little more outside of the box then it could have been. This led to a walk, frozen yogurt, and an evening drive on the island... Do you see the chain of events here? Making one little thing special led to an entire evening that became special. Rather than sitting at home and being bummed about cancelled plans, we turned our whole impromptu evening into one that we both truly enjoyed. My heart was filled to the brim with happiness.

In my first two years of sobriety, I spent a LOT of time alone. Let me tell you, when you have been the social butterfly of the party scene for years, staying home and not doing anything can start to feel almost depressing. It was so easy for me to feel lonely, like a total loser, and even depressed at times. I was so uncomfortable staying home and spending time by myself. It really started wearing on me over time and I realized I had to do something to change it.

I started this act of giving myself something to look forward to each day to help me get through the days. It was the only thing getting me through some of those days without a full blown episode of depression kicking in. Knowing that I was going to do something special at some point during my day was the ONLY highlight of my day sometimes. While this sounds really sad, it was something that helped to get me through the rough points. Putting the thing I gave myself to look forward to up on a pedestal each day was the light at the end of the tunnel that each day of my early sobriety had become. It really helped me get through the days without falling apart and slipping into that dark place of depression over and over again.

Try to think about the times in your life when things feel "routine" or like you are just going through the motions. It could be your morning workout. It could be your job. It could be the evenings of deciding what carryout to pick up. It could be staying in on a weekend night by yourself. Start to think of ways to change the way these things feel. What could you do to shake things up? What can you do to make these more typical things a little more exciting or special?

For myself, it was sometimes the tiniest things about my day that gave me something to look forward to. Anything that you can use to up-level or elevate your daily experience and your mood can be made into your something special for that day. It can be as simple as grabbing your favorite coffee from Starbucks during your errands or morning commute. It can be bigger like planning a girls' night out with your favorite friends. For some people it might be getting in bed early and watching a movie rolled up in the blankets. Never underestimate the power of getting in bed early, it's golden.

As I've stressed, I have a very love/hate relationship with working out if we're being completely honest. I don't love doing it. I like the way I feel afterwards, and I like seeing my body get stronger, but in the middle of a workout, I really just want it to be over. So how do I make it special? I like running outside. So I turn up good music or an audiobook and find somewhere that it visually pleasing to me. I give myself small goals to meet, and switch up what I do for a workout on any given day. I think about how I'll have the ability to zone out during my run. ME TIME! I pick out a new piece of workout clothing that makes me feel like I can run like a pro while looking super cute. I also visualize how strong and beautiful I will feel afterwards. I've got to make something new and unique about working out so that I am not wanting to scream by the end of it, but actually looking forward to it.

The same goes with work. I am lucky enough to be self-employed 90% of the time, but I do still work part-time at a waxing and cosmetic counter. I love the people I work with and I enjoy what I do, but I think we can all admit there are some days we would just rather stay home and do what we want instead of going to work. To make my two shifts a week at the counter stay enjoyable and exciting, I approach them in a way that does not feel like the same counter, for the same hours, with the same responsibilities every week. I use it as a chance to meet new people and hear their stories. Everyone has a story of their own to share. If you take the time to really ask someone about their day and their life, you'd be shocked at how many inspiring, strong people there are doing awesome things out there. I really try to focus on the experiences I am fortunate enough to have while working, and take away from them whatever I can in a positive way. This keeps things new and exciting at work for me because each day is a chance to meet new people and learn new things (It also doesn't hurt that I work with a bunch of beautiful, badass women too).

Even when I have the most routine, not-so-exciting day, I can transform it into one that is better by having my little something special planned for once I get home to relax that night. I'm not even kidding, sometimes I will visualize that later that night I will get into my comfiest comfies, light a candle, and cuddle with Kaya under a blanket while watching a chick flick on Netflix. That little visual of something I can look forward to makes the entire day a little bit brighter and happier. Try it.

When life gets busy, it is SO easy to let days become routine. Some days just seem like never ending emails, tasks, meetings, errands, and so on and so on. I get it... a lot of our daily tasks and responsibilities might not be super exciting. There is nothing about standing in line at the Secretary of State's Office that makes me light up inside. But sometimes there's just things we gotta do. We gotta get the little shit done too. Grind through it and check it off that check list so you can just get that much closer to something more enjoyable and special.

We all have so much on our plates on a daily basis that sometimes we let things become boring without even realizing it. We often push the things we do for ourselves out of the way because there is just too much to get done in one day. It can be overwhelming to even try to think about what you're going to do for yourself at the end of the day when you've got a million things to finish before the end of the day even comes. So maybe focusing on making the mornings more special is a better way for you to approach it (if this sounds like you). I've talked in my writing and on social media numerous times about how I started waking up an hour early to have more time for myself, but I want to emphasize the idea again here.

When I first started writing as a side hustle, I was already so busy that I had no idea how or when I was going to fit writing in regularly. Here I was with another one of my big dream goals, wondering how the hell I was ever going to have time to write an entire book with my already busy schedule. Typical me, I would not accept defeat. So I brainstormed ways to make it happen. I knew I was passionate about writing, and I knew how much I enjoyed it. I already had the idea in my pretty little head that I was going to write a book, so I was going to somehow get it accomplished one way or another.

By waking up an hour earlier every day, I was able to give myself at least an hour or more every morning to do something new that I was passionate about and enjoyed. One whole hour, uninterrupted and quiet, to focus on myself and my thoughts and get them onto the pages. It became liberating and inspiring first thing in the morning. It was like a mini therapy session every morning with myself. It changed my entire day.

I could feel myself blooming at the beginning of each morning just by making something about them a little bit more special. I had an entire block of time at the beginning of my day before all of the tasks and jobs for the day had the chance to get into my head and cloud it. It was my time. I began to look forward to it every day. I would wake up and make my coffee and then cuddle up with a blanket and my laptop (or at my desk if I wanted to feel more legit) and have my hour to let everything out and get myself balanced for my day. It made every day start out feeling WAY more special and positive. It made every day feel like an even better day.

So, I want to stress here how you can apply this idea to incorporate something into the start of your day that feels special just as I did with my writing if it seems like you just don't have the time at the end of your busy day. Maybe for you it would be easier to wake up a little earlier and do something for YOU before you do anything else in your day. Even though waking up earlier doesn't always sound like the greatest idea when the snooze button is tempting to hit several more times, it gives you the open free time in the morning to do something special for yourself at the beginning of your day. Just think about how different your entire day could start off if you did something to make it special first thing when you wake up. Think about the positive, happy tone you are setting for yourself for the next 24 hours by doing this. That first hour can hold some SERIOUS power.

I know sometimes my boyfriend laughs about how excited I get about the tiniest little things. He often laughs about how it's "so cute" when I verbally have to lay out our entire evening's plans when we aren't even going anywhere. Yes, I literally bounce up and down in the kitchen while I announce what I'm making for dinner in the slow cooker and that there is a new episode of *Bachelor In Paradise* on and that I grabbed two pints of peanut butter Halo Top (our fave) at the store for that night. This is probably another reason I love my Erin Condren planners so much. I love laying out my day or my week and hyping myself up for all the things I will be doing. It's literally just me trying to cover everything with an extra layer of excitement that makes them feel more special. Trust me, I'm such a pro at it now that I can sugar coat anything to make it seem more exciting. I can make any situation more fun, enjoyable, and special.

Think of it this way and try not to laugh. Think about when you were a little kid and your mom packed your lunch for school. If you're a mom already, think about your kids and how you pack their lunches. Peanut butter and jelly. Bag of carrot sticks. String cheese. Juice box. The basic go-to lunch blueprint for many parents... Now think about that same lunch transformed into one of those amazing themed Pinterest lunches where sandwiches have faces made out of thin sliced carrots and raisins to look like certain animals or characters. If you haven't seen these yet, seriously look them up. They are amazing. Parents get super into it. I literally just saw a lunch on Pinterest where a parent made a sandwich and veggie sticks into a full Thanksgiving turkey. But back to our basic idea here... Lunch could be a PB&J with the typical side items in baggies. But lunch could also be a fun little edible smiley face or dinosaur complete with dinosaur hard boiled eggs to accompany it. It could also have a little love note tucked inside with a reminder to have a good day.

Do you see my point here? Lunch was made a little more special by making little changes and upgrades. Imagine how you would feel opening that lunch as a kid next to Susie's plain old PB&J. You'd feel super special. You'd be excited for your lunch. Imagine how your kids feel when their friends gather around to see their lunch and wish they had a cool lunch like that too. You probably just made your kid's day a little bit more special. You go, Mom. See what I mean here? Make your life into the Pinterest lunch. Sure, it's easy to make the same old PB&J, but who wants PB&J when you can have a full Thanksgiving scene laid out in your lunchbox? (Okay, you can laugh now.)

Setting the tone of making things a little more special and exciting (when in reality they might not be) may seem silly at first. Some people might think I'm crazy when I talk about how hyped I am that I have Beef Stroganoff already cooking in my slow cooker and plan on getting into sweatpants and making my boyfriend rub my feet with lavender lotion while we watch *Teen Mom* when I get home at night. People might think it's "so cute" that I have to announce what I have in store for a Sunday off with the biggest smile on my face. I'm just making a conscious effort to make things in my life more special, which in turn, makes me happier every single day.

Let's start making the everyday, mundane days be anything but. Let's make each one of them a little more special. There is no reason why you can't make one thing about your day something that you can picture in your head and look forward to. Let it give you something to get a little excited about. Know that no matter how many boring little things you have in your day, you can always end or begin it with something a little special. Or you can cram it smack dab in the middle of your day if you need to. You can even make something you have to do that isn't exciting into something you can look forward to. It's all about shifting your mindset on things.

This idea of making every day special is really limitless, so start playing around with it! It gives you the opportunity to create your best life every day of your life, and who wouldn't want that? I incorporate this practice into every single day of my life and it truly shifts everything.

For example, I'm doing my final edits on this chapter while on a girl's weekend trip to Toronto. You might think that because I'm on a fun vacation that these days were already made special enough, right? Wrong. We did things every day on this trip that were not necessary and could be considered "extra," but they made it even more special and enjoyable. We got last minute tickets to see Janel Parrish in Grease the Musical at a beautiful theatre downtown, went to a super fancy traditional high tea, and even took the ferry ride from the city to Ward's Island just to ride in back and forth for thirty minutes straight. Did I mention we ate the most amazing food for four days straight as well? These were all extra things that weren't planned and maybe weren't necessary, but they truly up-leveled every day of our trip. We made every day of the trip a little bit more special, which just made us enjoy it even more.

You'll be shocked how much it can change your mood and your entire day by having one thing (or many things) to look forward to. You'll be shocked how it will make each day feel a little more special and a little more positive. It will make each day a little bit more happy. It will make each day one that you can get a little bit more excited about. In creating our best life possible, we should be able to get a little bit excited about it in the process. With all of the self-love, dating ourselves, and positive changes we are making so far, this one should be easy to start doing automatically.

So what can you make special about today? What can you up-level or upgrade in the next twenty-four hours to get excited about? I challenge you to get excited about the things you have to do today. Try it out and you will probably be surprised how having a positive mind-frame and getting excited about tiny things will boost your whole mood and your whole day. If nothing special is going on, then make something special! Create an opportunity to add something special to your life as often as you can. This one is totally dependent on your actions, your mindset, and the way you look at things, so get to it! Once you start to practice this regularly, you will innerbloom with even more happiness on a daily basis.

THINGS TO REMEMBER:

_____

_____

_____

_____

_____

_____

_____

_____

_____

_____

_____

_____

_____

_____

_____

_____

_____

_____

_____

_____

12 | WHAT MAKES YOU COME ALIVE

There is a quote from Howard Thurman that has always really hit home for me about finding your passion and your calling in life. I first heard this quote at least a decade ago, but it is still one of my favorites. The quote goes, "Ask yourself what makes you come alive and then go do that. Because what the world needs is more people that have come alive." How much more straight to the point can you really get than that? I applaud his bluntness in this quote because sometimes hearing something so directly is the way we really need to hear things to fully understand them. We don't need to hear the sugar-coated bullshit, we need to hear the truth. And Mr. Thurman just laid it out for us real nice and easy in plain black and white.

So what is it that makes your heart beat faster, makes your life feel more fulfilled, and makes you absolutely content inside? This is such a broad topic to hone in on that can really go in a million directions for any given person, kind of like a lot of others topics in this book can too. It's all about YOU. It really boils down to what YOU love doing, what YOU crave to do more of, and what YOU are truly passionate about. Honestly, think about what you love doing…

Think about something you would spend your time doing whether you were paid to do it or not. Think about something you would come home and spend time doing even if you just worked all day at your job. There are many people in the world that come home from an eight-hour work shift to work on something that they are passionate about. There are many people that wake up an hour early to work on a side hustle before they go to work for the day. If you are truly passionate about something, you make time for it no matter how tired or busy you are. We all have something that would make us want to do this. We all have something that we are truly passionate about that makes us come alive...

You know that feeling you get when something is truly meeting your needs and desires deep inside of you. Your heart feels full, your smile is natural and beaming, and you are just overflowing with love and warm happiness from the insides. We absolutely bloom from the inside when we are doing these things. These are the things that we love. These are the things we need to notice. What are you doing when you feel this way? Where are you when you feel this way? Who is around you when you feel this way? Start to take notice of the times that you truly feel alive inside.

Finding your path or your calling is something I have learned can be SO fulfilling. Sometimes when I think about the fact that I have gotten to this point right here, right now, it is difficult for me to put into words what it feels like inside. My heart overflows, my emotions pour out, and I can't even tell you how alive and truly happy and at peace I feel for the first time in my life. Each and every thing that has happened along the way has been lined up by God and the Universe to lead me right to here. Alive, enjoying my morning coffee on my balcony on a Sunday morning, and pounding away at the keyboard sharing my life's journey and story for everyone in the world to connect with. It's absolutely insane to me at times. If you would have ever told me in the past this is what I would be doing right now, I would have thought you were completely out of your mind. The hot mess express I used to be would have thrown back another shot and laughed at the idea of this life.

I recently finished reading *Light is The New Black* by Rebecca Campbell and I really sucked up every word she said about the resounding message in her book, "work your light." She elaborates in the book about working your light and discovering what your calling is, what your gift is, and what your purpose is... Finding that one thing that you would continue to do whether you were paid to do it or not. Finding the one thing that lights you up and chasing after it relentlessly. Finding that thing and working it. Working it until you feel yourself innerblooming. Working it not because you have to, but because you thoroughly and authentically enjoy it.

Have you ever stopped to think about what your true calling in life may be? If you have already discovered what yours is, good for you! You're already one step ahead. I probably couldn't have given you an answer as to what I thought my calling was up until recently. I knew I loved doing makeup. I knew I liked making YouTube videos. But was that really my bigger calling in the bigger picture of my life?

I would not for one minute give up any part of my makeup career because I am extremely passionate about it. I thrive off of being an entrepreneur and running my own business. I truly enjoy the things I do as my main career so much, but did they really fill up my heart and soul in a way that was almost indescribable at times? Did they really help me feel like I was reaching my bigger purpose in this life? Did I feel like I was sharing a gift from within myself with the world? Not as much as sharing my story through writing has done for me now.

The first time I realized that something made me feel more alive inside than I ever thought possible, I felt emotions completely overcome every part of me. This was the day I released *Sober as F****. Believe it or not, the day I released it on the anniversary of my two years of sobriety, I had one of the biggest anxiety attacks I've ever experienced in my life. The day was so overwhelming with emotions. It was almost crippling. If you've ever had an anxiety attack, you know what I'm talking about. Your chest feels full, you start breathing heavy, and your heartbeat races. The thoughts in your head are going out of control and it is hard to even think of anything else. I was absolutely freaking out, so I decided to go run it off on the treadmill. After I worked through it and calmed down, I realized that I was so overcome with emotion that I hadn't even known how to handle it. I had finally accomplished something HUGE with self publishing my first book. Everything was flooding in all at once. I was receiving tons of messages, I was frantically updating my blogs and websites, and I wasn't giving myself the time to process and actually take in what was happening.

I'm sure launching the book the day of my two year sober anniversary didn't help, but at the end of that day I felt more fulfilled than I ever have in my life. I had written a book. I HAD WRITTEN A F***ING BOOK. Never in a million years did I think I was capable of doing something like this. Within two weeks of the launch I had sold over 120 copies of the book online, was asked to do a podcast interview with one of my favorite authors, and was also asked to come speak to a women's group that meets locally in my area. It was like a complete and total whirlwind. WHAT WAS HAPPENING!? While it was a lot to take in and a lot all at once, it also felt like I was falling into exactly the place where I needed to be in my life for the first time.

When I discovered my calling of what I had always been meant to do, everything took shape authentically, organically, and completely on its own. The first time I fully accepted that I had discovered my calling was at that women's group I spoke at in a nearby city in Michigan. I was nervous as all hell and I hadn't even prepared anything ahead of time. I figured I would just wing it because, well, how could I screw up telling my own story? When I spoke at that meeting, the words poured out of me like I had done it many times before. My voice was not shaky, I didn't fumble on my words, and it just felt natural to me. I connected with a room of about fifteen to twenty women that I didn't even know. They asked me questions, they applauded my strength, and they supported what I was doing.

They hugged me, they congratulated me, and they told me that I had inspired them so much with my openness to share my story with them. I was overflowing with gratitude inside and I had never felt more alive.

At the end of the meeting, one of the women asked if the group could pray for me. I am a very spiritual and religious person so, of course, I said yes. We bowed our heads in a circle and a group of women I didn't even know prayed for me. They thanked God for keeping me alive at my rock bottom. They thanked God for giving me this message to share with and help others. I saw women I didn't even know before that night crying for me. Sitting in that circle praying, I have never felt anything like the feelings I felt at that moment. My eyes welled up in tears as a million emotions hit me all at once. My heart had never felt so full, I had never felt so much purpose, and I had never felt such an overwhelming sense of home. THIS was exactly where I was meant to be and I was doing exactly what I was meant to be doing... sharing the gift that was my story.

I know we all have read a million quotes on Pinterest and Instagram about how everything will always work out the way it is supposed to. I can actually say now that I believe every single one of those cute little quotes I've liked and shared on my pages about this idea. Looking back now, I can see how every little thing lined up just perfectly to bring me right here to this place in my life. The Universe had laid out this obstacle course of a life path for me to complete to reach this metaphorical winner's circle. Every little thing in my life was leading me here. I couldn't have planned it. I couldn't have forced it. I couldn't have prepared for it. It had to happen when and how it was supposed to happen.

Try to use this as a way to stop worrying about figuring out exactly where you should be right now or what you should be doing. I know doing this can be difficult. We have a tendency to be control freaks and want to know the outcome before we even embark on the journey. It's understandable because it can be a scary thing NOT knowing what lies ahead of you. It can be risky. It can be terrifying.

But try to put a little bit of faith in the idea of letting whatever will be, simply be. Try to take comfort in knowing that what is meant for your life will not pass your life. If something is meant to enter your life, then it will. If someone is destined to be a part of your life, then they will be. Let the Universe and God take the steering wheel and take you directly to where you should be and what you should be doing. You'd be surprised how simply it can happen. Be open to this type of spiritual guidance. Find your calling. Discover your light. Shine it bright.

Now before you go crazy quitting your job, selling everything you own, and embarking on some quest to discover what your calling is in life, try to look at your life now. Figure out what you need to do now to still be responsible when it comes to things like your finances. Try starting out by making small changes, because small changes can lead to BIG changes in the long run. Although YOU realize that you are trying to discover what your calling is, the bank won't care that you're "discovering what makes your come alive" when you quit your job and can't afford to make your car payment.

It may take some time, so be patient. It took me seven years of college, a Bachelor's Degree, a job teaching Preschool, a year in Beauty School, two failed blogs, years of mediocre quality YouTube videos, and months of trying to "figure out" what I was supposed to do before I even began to really figure any of it out at all. But I can say that every thing I did along the way was a part of the journey when I look back on it. I don't see the years I spent in college, the multiple jobs I worked, and the failed first attempts at writing as bad things. I don't see them as being of waste of time. I see them as learning experiences and opportunities to grow within myself. I see them as stepping stones leading to a bigger destination.

To be completely honest with you, I worked seven days a week and busted my ass for years to get to where I am now. I had to stay smart about making career changes in my life and do them responsibly. Would it be nice to just flip the middle finger to your unfulfilling job and horrible boss and embark on your quest of finding out what makes you feel complete? Sure. Is it realistic to actually do that? Usually the answer is no. Because we are adults and we have responsibilities and bills (unfortunately).

Sometimes you've got to put in the work to get to the place where you will no longer feel like its work. Make sure you are financially being safe and start exploring a side hustle. That's exactly how I figured out what I was meant to do. I taught preschool during the week and did makeup all weekend for years until I was actually ready to make the switch into being a full time makeup artist the smart and responsible way. When I finally did it, I couldn't have been happier.

When I first started writing *Sober as F****, I would wake up an hour earlier everyday, like I have mentioned already, just to fit in writing time for months on end before I started working for the day. Now that the book is done and I've officially been selling a self-published book on Amazon, it's been the most fulfilling thing I've ever done. The early mornings and the extra hours of working at home were all worth it in the end. You see, it's not always easy along the way. Sometimes it's a ton of extra work, but I can tell you that the work is definitely worth it. All of the purposeful and hard work will pay off big time in the long run.

When you find your calling or your purpose, things will feel like they are just finally making sense. You will feel like you've finally discovered the answer to a question you didn't even know you were asking. Something will just click and feel complete. I have noticed that I no longer feel as stressed about getting a million things done, I can enjoy some actual down time, and I have a newfound sense of accomplishment. I just feel like I've arrived at where I am supposed to be right now. I feel like I've finished a long journey. Having that sense of comfort and ease inside is indescribable. This feeling is how I know that I was meant to reach this point.

I always felt like I was still working, still changing things, still trying to figure out my next move. I always felt like there was something more that I should be doing. I felt like nothing was ever done or enough in my heart. I constantly felt like I was on the verge of a breakthrough but never actually got to that point. For once in my life, I don't feel that way. I feel as if I have landed in just the right spot and I am ready to ride it out from here now. I have faith that the Universe and God will put whatever is meant to be next directly in front of me exactly when it needs to be there. I can finally exhale. I can finally feel like I'm HOME.

Because I am not the type of girl to ever be "finished" with anything, I am already brainstorming what my next move will be with my calling. Something has been stirring up inside of me to expand my writing to the next level. While discovering a few new blogs and podcasts recently, I have stumbled on a few that have left me feeling inspired and hungry to do more again. So the other day, I bought my own name as a domain name. Right now I have it redirecting people to my current blog, SoberAF.com, but I've got some plans I'm stirring up in my little head for what I am going to do with it. I know sharing myself and my story with others makes me feel so fulfilled and good inside, and I want to take it to the next level. It's going to be a lot of work and a huge project, but I am planning on creating a central location for my readers, my Youtube followers, and my friends on my own personal website and blog. By the time you actually have this book is in your hands, sarahordo.com will be up and running! So feel free to hop on over and check it out. (wink, wink.)

After feeling how my first blog and book made me feel so alive and complete inside, I knew that I wanted to keep working in this direction. I know that creating this new website and blog will bring everything I share together into one spot for people to be a part of. I know that I want to share more of my life and my story with the world for people to connect with. This is what makes me come alive. So I want to dive into it with my whole heart. I know that what I do now fills my heart up and gives me true inner happiness. It makes me feel fulfilled. It makes me want to do more. It makes me feel like I am unstoppable. It makes me feel like I am in full bloom inside.

Don't you want to feel this? To feel like you have found

something that you are so passionate about that you can't wait to jump in head first. You deserve to know how amazing this feels. You deserve to know what it's like to find something that feeds your heart and soul and makes you want to do more of it. You deserve to create your best life and feel what its like to bloom.

This idea reminds me of an episode of Cara Alwil Leyba's *Style Your Mind* podcast about creating your dream world and your fantasy life. The whole idea in this message was to create the world you want to live in. Create the situation you want to be in. Create the environment you want to surround yourself with. Make everything so on par with what makes you feel alive that it feels like a dream at times. Make what you are doing in life something you are passionate about every day. Discover your calling and do something that you can't believe you are lucky enough to be doing.

After I heard this podcast it was like a lightbulb went on in my head. I've talked about how at times it is almost indescribable how fortunate and happy I feel about how my life is going now. I couldn't be happier. I couldn't feel more blessed for the life I am living. That was the moment that I realized that this is exactly what I did… I created my dream world. I turned my life into one that felt like a daydream or a fantasy. I made every little thing that happened happen. I was responsible for getting myself here. I am the reason I am doing what I am doing. I changed my life. I started the blog. I posted the videos. I wrote the book. If I had the power to do this and discover my calling by finding the things that would make me feel truly alive and happy, then you absolutely can too.

So start to find the things that make you come alive. Even if you don't plan on dropping everything and chasing after your craziest dreams just yet, take some baby steps. Start that blog you've been thinking about. Look into going back to school to have your dream career. Start a Pinterest board with inspirational photos. Do what you can to start walking in the direction of finding out what you are passionate about in your life. If you already know what it is, dive into it head first! Work will feel less like work and more like a passion.

You won't dread thinking about going to your job every Monday. You will feel a purpose and a passion for what you are doing like never before. You will be able to accomplish so many things. The sky is the limit honey, and there is no glass ceiling here.

THINGS TO REMEMBER:

13| MONEY, SUCCESS, FAME, GLAMOUR

We all love things that sparkle and shine. A new car, a new diamond, new clothes, and a beautiful new house are all things that we understandably enjoy. And who wouldn't want these things, honestly? We work because we need money, and we need money to buy the things that we need (or just plain want). Having things around us that make us happy is just a way of life. We buy the things we like. We splurge on the nice things that we desire. I am in no way trashing this idea, because I own a lot of things that I saved up to splurge on that some people would call unnecessary. Guilty as charged. So unless you plan on selling everything you own and living a true minimalist lifestyle, it's important to find your balance here. Of course we are going to want to go shopping for new clothes, to get the newest technology-driven phone or toy out there, and obviously we'd love to have that fancy new convertible... but we need to find a balance here.

The important thing to identify is that we are not relying on these outside things to be our primary source of happiness or the answer to our problems in life. We are very materialistic people in today's world, and there is no doubt about that. People today have more unnecessary shit than ever before. We're brainwashed daily that we need to have the newest, the biggest, and the best of EVERYTHING in life. Some people tend to place a very high priority on things like how much money they have and how many nice things they own. These things can definitely make us happy, but it is so crucial to make sure they are not the things taking priority in determining our true inner happiness in our everyday lives.

Don't get me wrong, we need money to have shelter, to have food to eat, and to take care of our daily needs. We are not about to go and sell all of our things and "live off the land" in our suburban neighborhoods. So, yes, we do need money for a lot of things. But how many of us are attaching such an importance and power to money that we are allowing it to dictate our happiness in our lives? We've all heard the phrase "Money can't buy happiness," but I think we all know that it sure can help at times. This is why money is the root of a lot of issues in life. Stressing about money is unfortunate, and sometimes it can feel just plain unavoidable altogether. Money is the root of many problems and messes, and it even has the power to dramatically crack the foundation of some marriages and relationships.

There have been at least several times in my life where money has caused problems and stress that I can easily identify. Not having enough money to get the newer used car that I wanted after being in a car accident (where my car was totaled) was one of them. Not being able to get a mortgage or be pre-approved to buy a home was another time. I remember sitting in my car crying after I had been denied for a mortgage because of my self-employment. Talk about a hard blow to your big, exciting plan you've dreamed up for your life. When money (or a lack of money) throws a wrench in your life and makes things difficult, it sucks. It sucks that a bunch of thin pieces of paper can actually have that much power and influence over you and so many things in your life.

You may not have the biggest house on the block. You may not have the most expensive car. You may not have the designer handbags. But are you living? Are you breathing? Do you have friends and family that love you regardless of what you have? These are the important things. Money and belongings will never buy you true love. They will never buy you authentic self-confidence or faith in yourself. They will never buy you true and entire inner happiness and peace. Money will never truly make you bloom from the inside. If we could just swipe a card and make life perfect, we would have all already done that years ago. Life is not about the money and the things, it is more so about the people and the experiences we live in it. Always remember that.

We all want to be successful in life. Who wants to actually fail at things? Nobody. Nobody wakes up and thinks 'I really hope I totally bomb this project at work today.' We all want to nail the interview, get recognized for our accomplishments, and have success in everything that we do. It makes us feel proud of all the hard work we put into the things that we do. We like our photo to be put up on the employee of the month board, if you will. Unless you are somebody that hates having attention on you, most of us thrive off of our accomplishments and being recognized for them. It just feels plain good to achieve something and have someone give you a little pat on the back for a job well done. We love being acknowledged for our hard word and the things we do well. It just makes us feel good.

I will be the first one to acknowledge that when you feel like you aren't doing as well as you think you should be doing, it can really be a blow to your self confidence. Nobody wants to feel like a failure. Nobody wants to not succeed at the goals they set for themselves. Nobody wants to be unable to reach the dreams they have for their life. Nobody wants to feel like they just aren't doing well enough. It sucks. It drags you down. It has the power to steal all of your happiness.

Leaving a stable teaching job to pursue being an entrepreneur was a huge risk for me to take in life. And I'll be honest with you, there was a point where I was scared as s***. If you are (or have considered being) an entrepreneur, you probably know what I am talking about. There is no stable paycheck, there is no company matching your 401k contributions, there is no health insurance, and your success is completely dependent on YOU. Entrepreneurship isn't cut out for everyone, and that is totally fine. But for those of us that do find ourselves chasing that goal in life, success can be SO fulfilling. It made me feel more accomplished than anything else ever had in my entire life. Just remember that starting your own thing and being your own boss will most likely come along with a lot of bumps in the road, mistakes, and failures to learn from. Be ready for them.

I used to always want to hide those things I considered to be failures in my own life. I was guilty of being one of those girls that only put the highlight reel of their life on their Facebook and Instagram page. I never wanted people to see that I struggled, failed, and was anything but the perfect picture I portrayed myself to be on a daily basis. I never wanted to look weak, like I needed the help of others, or like I couldn't do the things I set my mind to on my own. But things really changed for me when I started to see the things I considered to be my "failures" or "flaws" in a completely different light.

Failing at things is NOT a bad thing. I repeat, failing at things is NOT a bad thing. Without our failures, we would never learn valuable lessons and grow in life. Without screwing something up at some point, we would never learn how to do it differently the next time around. Our failures and the things we do not succeed at can prove to be some of the biggest learning and growth opportunities we will ever have in our entire lives. Look at your failures as tiny little bits of silver wisdom covered with tarnish. They look ugly. They are undesirable. Nobody wants the tarnished piece of silver jewelry when it looks like that. But once it is cleaned, it is shiny and valuable. Now everyone wants it. Think of the things you don't succeed at as these pieces of silver. They still hold value even though they were once seen as undesirable junk. Clean away the tarnish of your failures to find the value that still rings true underneath, because that is where the true value lies.

Learning from your past and gaining new knowledge from the things you did not succeed at is so important to our inner well-being. We must forgive ourselves for our failures, and acknowledge the fact that we won't always be the best at everything. Someone will always be better than you. Someone will always be more successful than you. Someone will always have more than you. That's just a fact of life. So do not be hard on yourself for the things you fail at or the things you are not the best at. Take what you have done and learn from it. Use it to learn and to grow as a person.

We all make mistakes and we all f*** up. That's life. So while we all strive to be successful all of the time, go easy on yourself when you fail. It's one of the most valuable opportunities for knowledge and growth that you will ever have. So in reality, we should actually be thankful for our failures.

Take the lessons you receive from every struggle and every failure in your life and use them to learn. Use them to gain valuable knowledge. Use them to grow. Let your struggle build you into someone who is hardworking, resilient, and can take anything life throws at him/her in stride. When you learn to roll with the punches, life becomes SO much easier. Once you accept the idea that things will not always go perfectly, the sun won't always shine, and you will fail at something at some point in your life, you will feel so much better. If we let every little struggle and failure convince us that we are not good enough, we will never be successful in life. We are good enough. We can all be successful in life. If we let every little thing that goes wrong ruin our day, we will never enjoy all of the beautiful moments we have the opportunity to live in.

I have f***ed up SO many times in my life. Seriously, I have really made some big messes. I have failed at a lot of things. I've made a lot of dumb choices. I've willingly put myself in a lot of dangerous situations. I have totaled cars, been kicked out of college classes, gotten myself into money problems, and drank myself into the emergency room. But what I can say is that I have learned from each failure, each mess, and every f*** up.

So stop trying to be perfect. Be messy. Make mistakes and f*** things up. It's okay to show that you are flawed and that you have failed at things. Nobody is perfect. The sooner we realize this and stop putting such a crazy amount of pressure on ourselves to be perfect at everything 24/7, the sooner we will be able to relax a little bit. The sooner we can do this, the sooner we will be able to look at our failures in a more positive light.

Of course the goal is to be successful, but you've got to accept the fact that you won't always succeed 100% of the time. Use it to learn and grow from it. Show others that it is okay to not be successful and succeed all the time. This will help to show others that it's okay to fail. Your new and more positive attitude towards your failures and flaws may even help others to feel this way to. Positivity rubs off on people, so start putting out some more positive vibes when it comes to failing at things.

Of course, success can be SO fulfilling. I can't even begin to explain to you how amazing it feels to share the things I have been successful at in my life with the world. I know it's not polite to brag, but sometimes you just have to brag! When you have been working so hard, grinding everyday, and reaching tiny successes, sometimes you have to just have a little brag session and acknowledge your own hard work. You deserve it! Give your self a little pat on the back and a big round of applause. We need to start acknowledging all the work we do more often. Nobody is gonna hate on you for doing this. And if they do.. F*** em. Nobody needs that kind of negativity in their life when they are on the road to finding true happiness and blooming from the inside. And there's no room for those people who don't want the best for you when you are creating your best life anyways.

It's like when you're creating your profile on a dating website. Nobody puts in their Tinder profile that they lost a job, have a ton of student loan debt, or have a serious fear of commitment. That would lead to a whole lot of left swipes. We share our accomplishments, the things we are good at, and what we consider to be the best qualities about ourselves. So do I tell the world that it took me about seven years to complete my bachelor's degree in college? Hell no. Do I shout from the rooftops that I have had a horrible track record when it comes to dating and relationships? Only in my books (LOL).

But seriously, do not feel guilty for sharing your triumphs and successes in life. You are not bragging, you are just showing yourself a little bit of love for all of your hard work. When you have been working your ass off for everything you have or have done in your life, you deserve to be able to brag just a little bit. Just remember, don't be an asshole. Always stay HUMBLE.

At one point in my journey, I noticed at times that I would feel kind of like an asshole if I shared too many accomplishments of mine publicly. I never wanted to be one of those "LOOK AT ME AND HOW GREAT I'M DOING" type of people on social media. I always tried to keep it modest. I often felt this way the most if I was dating someone who was struggling. I didn't want to excitedly share every one of my accomplishment and goals that I met to them and make them feel bad. RED FLAG. While it's okay not to want to hurt someone else's feelings, I should have never put myself in a situation where I felt bad for being proud of myself and the things I had done. Never put yourself in an environment where you feel like you need to dull down what you're worth and what you've built for yourself at the cost of someone else's ego.

I've always loved the quote about "watch to see who claps when you're doing well" and I find it to be so true. I have seen in my own previous friendships and relationships that some people just can't handle when other people are doing better than them. This is such a twisted feeling to process. I had to remind myself many times that when people are unhappy and unsupportive of your successes it is only because they are unhappy with something in their own lives. I had to reassure myself that I was doing absolutely nothing wrong by being successful, but that they were the ones struggling to be happy with the person they are and with the life they are living. These kinds of negative people were the ones that fortunately fell away on their own over time as I grew and bettered myself as a person. It can be extremely sad and disappointing, but when you are doing the self-work and reflection to find everything you need within you to be truly happy, sometimes it just has to happen.

Now if you've ever watched the 80s movie *Party Monster* with Macaulay Caulkin, you may have picked up right away that the title of this chapter came directly from a song featured in that movie. If you've never seen it, you should probably go watch it because it is like every former club kid's (like myself) extreme autobiography. For a long time, I thought I needed to have this glamorous lifestyle on the outside that looked desirable to others to be happy on the inside. I thrived off of the attention and the false sense of happiness that it gave me. I thought that I was the shit. But at the end of every weekend I was still the same girl with the same issues and the same problems in life. Getting a ton of attention and oozing a glamorous lifestyle didn't solve any of my real problems or issues I needed to fix inside of myself.

If you were friends with me on Facebook or Myspace years ago (really aging myself with that one), you would have seen a montage of myself in tight skirts, bra tops, Amy Winehouse teased hair, glassy eyes, and posing on Detroit warehouse street corners. 95% of those photos would feature a water bottle filled with vodka or a drink in my hand. I would wear big coordinated bows in my hair or a flashy headband going around my forehead like a ninja. I always wore thigh-high boots or sky high heels. I was a f***ing disaster, and I thought I looked great... I looked like a baby hooker.

I LOVED putting photos like this everywhere because I thought that everyone wanted my glamorous lifestyle of the lush I saw myself as. The whole reason I put them out there for everyone to see was exactly for that reason... I wanted everyone to see me. I had such a warped idea of self-worth that was directly related to how much attention I got from others on a regular basis. Throughout my teens and my young adult life, I connected attention with being good enough. I connected attention with being happy. How sad is that? I'm so thankful I have overcome this stage in my life and changed everything around for the better. Imagining myself posing on top of a toilet at the bar drunk with big hair and a water bottle of vodka right now having my friends take thirteen photos of me makes me absolutely cringe. Nothing about that is cute.

Some people spend their entire lives chasing after their 15 minutes of fame thinking that once they get that kind of attention, everything will change. It might. It might get better for a while. It might get way worse. Who knows? It's almost as if we relate the fame and attention associated with celebrity status as some sort of approval. The underlying idea here is that by doing this we are searching for validation in ourselves and in our lives from outside factors and people. We are letting other people dictate if we are good enough, to put it bluntly. We are letting other people tell us if we are thin enough, if we are pretty enough, if we are successful enough, and if we have enough.

Look at any tabloid in the checkout at your local Target… Khloe Kardashian gained 20 pounds. Ben Affleck cheated on Jennifer Garner. Here's 20 celebrities without makeup on being rated by how bad they look. It's freakin' brutal out there in the public eye. I don't know about you, but I would never want to be plastered on the cover of one of those magazines showing the world how I have cellulite when I wear a bikini at the beach (newsflash: EVERYONE does).

Obviously by writing, having a blog, and doing YouTube videos, I let a lot of people into my life. Don't think for a second that I haven't experienced the judgement tenfold already. People have told me that they think I look like a man without makeup on. People have told me that I should go get a nose job. People have told me that I sound dumb when I talk in my YouTube videos. Someone even told me once they "had to turn the video off because it sounded like nails on a chalkboard"… People are horrible. Seriously. People have called me out for the wrinkles I have starting on my forehead and told me that I should go get Botox. People have called my problems with alcohol "not a real addiction" on my YouTube videos. When you put yourself out there in a public way, everyone is going to have an opinion about you and what you're doing.

Now the point I want to make is that if you are doing or are going to do something where any amount of "fame" and attention may be drawn to you, get ready. A lot of us may think that we want it, but a lot of things can come along with it. First of all, having lots of attention on yourself is not going to solve any of your problems. It may make you feel important and special temporarily, but it's not going to solve any of your deeper problems in life. You might face a lot of criticism. You might face a lot of judgement. And that can wreck true havoc on your self-esteem and confidence inside of you.

I try to take the negativity and the hate comments and brush them off. I laugh about some of them because, honestly, these people are taking time out of their day to try to bring you down.. for what? Don't they have anything better to do? Guess not. Brush it off, because you don't have the time to waste on that. Unhappy people only unleash negativity because they are unhappy with themselves, bottom line. It has nothing to do with you.

The best way to get through this is to surround yourself with positive people that support everything you are doing in life. There are a lot of people that will clap for you and support what you are doing. This is what we want to welcome into our lives. This will make us feel happy and successful with everything we are doing. I know that I love sharing my successes in female empowerment groups on Facebook because there are thousands of my own personal cheerleaders that are just one post away. I know I've mentioned these groups a million times in my writing, but I seriously love these groups so much. There are a million people out there just looking to support others and to be supported in return. And this can make you feel amazing inside. Take advantage of it.

Finding true inner peace and happiness cannot be attained by simply having money and buying lots of things. Having lots of material things cannot fill us up and make us feel content if we aren't already happy on the inside. Having fame and lots of attention won't ever fulfill all of the needs of our inner self. Having a glamorous life won't answer all of our problems. Sure, we can enjoy all of these things being a part of our life, but make sure you don't ever impose so much importance on them that they dictate your happiness in life.

It's important to find a balance within yourself when it comes to these things. True inner happiness can definitely be influenced by things like money, success, fame, and glamour, but it can't dictate it entirely. We will never truly innerbloom if we are constantly obsessing over how much money we have, how much fame we attain, how many times we succeed or fail, and how glamorous our life looks to others. That is why it is SO crucial that we don't attach too much importance on these things while truly working to create our best life possible.

THINGS TO REMEMBER:

14 | SELF-SOOTHING

I know that in the past when I get uncomfortable, anxious, or face difficult things, I have always wanted to lean on other people or things as a coping mechanism, specifically alcohol and men. In the past when things would be going wrong, I would be in full retreat mode inside of my townhouse on a Thursday night and I would be hurting. I would be feeling lost. I would be questioning a lot of things about where I am in my journey. I am struggling to sit there for that evening alone. A million thoughts would run through my head of who I could call, who I could vent to, and even the thought of inviting someone over to distract myself. I would be wanting to go out and get wasted to forget about whatever it was making me upset. I would be sitting thinking of how I could possibly distract myself and ignore these feelings rather than actually feel them and deal with them. At one point, this would have been the point that I went to the bar and drank my emotions away, because God knows it was much easier to throw back shots and drown away my consciousness and problems with vodka than to actually face them.

THIS was not healthy, and I know that. So what am I doing differently about it now? I am forcing myself to self-soothe. It is hard. It is so foreign to me. It is difficult. But I am forcing myself to feel every bit of emotions, to understand them, and to work through it in a healthier way. Being able to do this is so crucial to finding yourself and everything you need to be happy when things are not going easy. It would be simple for me to just give in to something familiar like I used to that I know would temporarily comfort me, but we're not taking the easy way out. Not this time.

Just as parents allow their babies to cry so that they learn how to soothe themselves, that it what I have been doing here and now in my life. I am forcing the sometimes delicate, child-like, emotional young woman traveling along the journey of finding true happiness to learn how to self-soothe again. I am an adult. Nobody is going to hold me and rock me to sleep. Nobody is going to bring me a warm bottle to quiet my hunger. I've got to take matters into my own hands now. I had to learn how to soothe myself on my own.

Just as a small infant does when they self-soothe, I must learn to do this too as a young woman. I need to face the uncomfortable feelings and things in my life and learn to soothe myself back to a peaceful and comfortable state. We all need to learn how to do this because it is such a healthy practice in life. Harnessing the control to nurse yourself back to a peaceful state of mind when things aren't going smoothly is such a mighty gift. In doing so, you will have the power to overcome the negative thoughts, the comforting bad habits, and the short term solutions to our everyday problems in our lives. This is going to make things SO much easier along the way.

Things will get rough on this journey. When you are striving to cut off all of the unnecessary things from your life on the outside, there will be many things that you may feel you NEED or CAN'T give up simply out of habit and comfort. There are probably a lot of external factors in your life that you have leaned on throughout the years when things are not going right, when the road gets twisted and bumpy, and when you need something that feels familiar. We've all done it throughout our lives. We all have a bad habit of finding comfort in and relying on things that feel safe or make us feel better quickly and easily. We can basically call it a "vice" of sorts. Something we rely on and revisit often out of pure comfort or pleasure, even though we know it is not always good for us. My vice used to be alcohol in extremely large amounts and letting in shitty men that didn't truly care about me.

Just as those that have a vice of drugs or alcohol do, we seek the comfort of something familiar. Something to temporarily make us feel good. Something to block out the things we don't want to face or deal with. We would much prefer something that can give us the good feelings for now and a feeling of instant gratification when we desire it. It's another easy answer. Quick and easy. But this is the hard part and the biggest fight in finding true self-love and inner peace. This is where the hard work and one of the biggest battle lies in our journey of finding everything we need within ourselves. It's time to acknowledge our vices. It's time to point out the external things we turn to or lean on for a temporary and instant "fix" of sorts. It's time to find our inner strength to change our patterns into healthier ones.

What do you turn to in times of chaos, discomfort, and unfamiliarity? Do you reach for a cigarette to light up for a fix? Do you just need a drink to take your mind off of the stress? Do you search out the sexual attention of others when you feel insecure and low? Pinpoint your vice (or vices, if you have many). 99.9% of the time, in my experience, your vice will be something that is not always healthy, or that offers short-time fulfillment only. You can easily smoke the cigarette, drink the bottle of wine, and sleep with the booty call. Instant gratification. You instantly feel better. But give it five minutes. Give it an hour. Give it a day. What now? Another cigarette, another bottle, another emotionless romp? Do you feel better? Is everything fixed? Did your vice solve all of the underlying problems you struggle with in your life? Doubtful. Very doubtful.

Self-soothing can be hard when it is something new and foreign to you. Everything in your head is SCREAMING at you to turn to the familiarity of the vice. You might even entertain the thought of it in your head and temporarily think it is a good answer to the problems at hand.

I am still learning to master this whole act of self-soothing. For as long as I can remember, I had turned to my external vices in an attempt to solve all of my issues. This makes it an extremely hard habit to break. This makes it feel like a literal internal war inside of your head when you start trying to cut off these things you have turned to so much and for so long. You will most likely want to go back to the familiar things you once turned to for an easy "answer" to all of your problems. Old habits die hard, remember?

Once you have been able to identify what your vices are, you will probably still want to turn to them like they are an old friend. You may even romanticize the idea of indulging in them again. I did this a lot with alcohol during my first year sober. I played with the idea numerous times of thinking that one day I'd be able to drink in a normal, healthy way again.

I used to picture myself on a beautiful, tropical beach somewhere soaking up the sun with my husband on our honeymoon with a coconut drink in hand. I would imagine myself on a fancy trip to Europe where I would sip on a glass of local wine and savor the whole experience while exploring. I know I am better off without alcohol. I've been sober now for over two years with no plans to drink again anywhere in sight. That's just how a vice works. It creeps in and lingers in the back of your mind sometimes and taunts you with the pleasurable aspect of letting it back in. Not today, vice. Not today.

It's time to start saying no. It's going to be a struggle and it's going to take time. I can tell you that throughout my first year sober, things would weigh very heavily on me emotionally and mentally. But I started fighting it. And at some point I was no longer weak to my vices. You have more inner strength and will power inside of you than you even know of, you just need to discover it. When you fully commit to kicking your vices and no longer turning to the quick fixes, you will be amazed at the strength you realize you have had within you all along. I feel like freakin' Superwoman at times when I really sit back and think about how far I've come with my relationship with alcohol. My newfound inner strength and will power allowed me to go from an Emergency Room with IVs and sensors all over my body to self-publishing a book about my sobriety…. All because I decided to fight off my vices and my addictions and to better my life.

If you face an actual "addiction" with your vices, please be well aware that it may be a little more difficult to fight them. You may need help. Although I was able to kick the alcohol itself, I was a disaster emotionally and mentally while doing so. When you remove something that has been an addictive piece of your puzzle for a long time, it's going to be a bit of work. I am no doctor, but I do want to make the point that you should 100% be able to look for and accept help to rid yourself of these things if you need it. Removing something that has been an addiction is going to shake your whole world up, so get ready.

I know there are a million debates about whether an addiction is a "choice" or a "disease" in a million articles, books, and blogs. I'll let you decide what you think it is, but as someone who has been through it… I can firmly say that to me addiction IS a disease. All day. Every day. You may choose to use whatever you are addicted to when you are in the throes of a full blown addiction, sure. But now in sobriety, I can look back and tell you that people don't cause that much hurt and that much pain to themselves and to the people that care about them like it's just a choice or a flip of a coin. When you are suffering from addiction, you are sick. When you are sick, you can't always be intentional about what happens. It wasn't a heads or tails decision or a choice for me to consume that lethal cocktail of alcohol and drugs and almost take away my mother's baby girl from her. Sorry. I don't believe it for a second.

Seek out the help that will be best for you to overcome your addiction. For myself, that included Church, one-on-one therapy, self-development books and podcasts, and changing everything about my life. If you read my first book then you know that I tried to do it cold turkey, with no help, and on my own for quite some time at first. But

I can tell you now that I only wish I knew then what I know now when I first walked into that battle. There is so much help and support out there for kicking addictions, you just have to be willing to accept it. So ask for it. Use it. Work it. It will make things so much easier.

Turning away from your vices (or addictions) will force you to acknowledge this newfound inner strength, but will also stir up many other feelings and emotions inside. If you need to, break down, crack, and feel the pain. Feel the uncomfortable feelings and fully bask in them. As I've said before, nothing good happens in your comfort zone. We're pushing through a very uncomfortable place and doing the work to learn and grow from it. The times we feel the most uncomfortable and the most overwhelmed in life are the times we make our greatest strides and gain the most priceless knowledge. The difficult things we go through are the things that teach us the most, so start taking some serious notes here.

Self-soothing… How do we do it? First of all you're going to have to feel the uncomfortableness. Most people try to avoid getting to this point, because nobody wants to face their demons. Nobody likes feeling uncomfortable. It's hard. It's tiring. It makes you realize things about yourself that may not be so pretty. Feel every second of it. Are you uncomfortable? Are you anxious? Are you hurting inside? Feel it all. Do you want to turn to something to just make it all go away? Would that be the easy way out? Put on your battle gear, Wonder Woman, because we are fighting through it this time.

Let's first acknowledge that something has triggered something inside of us that we don't like. We are the crying baby screaming out for someone (or something) to come in and soothe us. Unlike the baby, we don't really need someone to bring us food, rock us, and change our diaper (unless you're into that type of thing… but, ew). How do you quiet a crying baby? You give them something. A pacifier, a bottle, attention… So how do we soothe ourselves here now that we are feeling some unpleasant emotions? THIS is the time we typically turn to our vices and our addictions, the things that are familiar to us. The things that will comfort us temporarily. The quick fix. The short term solution. So here is where we start to change things up.

Let yourself feel what you're feeling. Take a moment to acknowledge what has triggered this emotional response. What is upsetting you? What is bothering you? I'll use my past as an example. I used to always let the wrong men in too much, too soon. They'd usually give me a clue pretty quickly that I might not be able to trust them. I knew something wasn't right or healthy, but I'd still follow my old ways. I fell back into my old patterns again and again. I would feel just like a record stuck on repeat. WHY couldn't I just stop being that way with men? It always led to my feeling terrible at the end of it. Why did I keep doing the same things over and over again and expect a different outcome to happen?

This was the moment I would re-download Tinder. I would swipe right and start meaningless conversations with men in an attempt to show myself that I could just find someone else. This is when I'd respond to that late night text, because this other guy is familiar and I know he likes seeing me. This is when I would immediately block this guy out and find the next one, telling myself I would start over and do things differently the next time around. Today, I'm no longer doing any of these things. I am now identifying and acknowledging the way I am feeling, and why I am feeling that way. Clearly my past vice of men was never the answer to my bigger problem, which was really my self-worth.

So what I started doing at times like these was putting the phone down. Deleting Tinder. Not reaching out to anyone else. I would acknowledge that I was going to play it differently that time around. I would self-soothe instead. I would show myself a little bit of self-love and self-care. I no longer would beat myself up over it. I would light a candle, relax, and reflect. I'd listen to some music, maybe watch a movie, or maybe do some reading. I also started giving myself a little pat on the back for not turning to my usual vice again. Make sure you acknowledge any little baby steps you make like this because the bottom line is, you're making changes. You're trying. You're making an effort to do the work.

Self-soothing is all about feeling what you're feeling, acknowledging what you're feeling, and learning how to make yourself calm down on your own. Just like the baby that will cry until they fall asleep or realize that crying is no longer getting them the response they wanted. Mom isn't coming to rock them back to sleep. Even though they are upset and crying, the baby is forced to soothe themselves and calm themselves down. That is exactly what we are doing. We are calming ourselves down. We are acknowledging that something has triggered or upset us, and we are working to get ourselves back to our own state of inner peace and happiness.

Sometimes when I'm feeling anxious or upset I like to use mantras. This is very new to me as I am still getting familiar with all of this yoga, meditation, and spiritual stuff on a deeper level. Meditation is still weird to me, but I'm working on it. One of my favorite mantras I like to say to myself a few times when I can feel my anxiety rising or something has triggered my emotions is "You are in control. You are fine. You've got this." Sometimes I just have to remind myself that I am in control of what is happening within myself. I have to tell myself that whatever is happening isn't going to kill me, it's going to pass. I am going to be absolutely fine. This too will pass, just like everything else does. I've got this.

It's insane how shifting your mindset and the thoughts in your head can shift your entire situation. If you let the inner voice of your ego and self-doubt dominate, it's going to do just that... dominate. It's going to consume your thoughts and convince you that things are going wrong and that you should be reacting to them. Thoughts like "You really screwed this one up" or "This is gonna get really bad" will only work you up more and surround you with even more negativity. When you surround yourself with negative thoughts and words, you're going to drag yourself down with them. It's like a breeding ground for negativity. It's time to put on your positive pants.

Surrounding yourself with positivity will work wonders when it comes to self-soothing yourself. If we want to feel happiness inside, we need to stop surrounding ourselves with and focusing on the negatives. So find every little way to add a little more positivity into your life when thing are rocky. Attempt to shift your mindset and the way you look at what is bothering you. When I am able to do this, I can look at an unfavorable situation in a much different way and work through it much easier. You are what you surround yourself with. So when you are faced with something difficult, surround yourself with LOTS of positivity to get past it.

You are in total control of your inner most emotions. The things you do, the things you surround yourself with, and the way you think will all directly affect your ability to self-soothe. You harness the ability to soothe any unpleasant feeling or emotions inside of you. You are in control of your thoughts and emotions way more than you think. We often automatically think that our outside factors in our life determine way more about our feelings, our emotions, and our mindset than they actually do. They only have that power over us if we let them have that control. They only have the ability to do this because we allow them to. So let's shift our mindsets a bit to realize that we are in control of our happiness way more than we may have originally thought. We can always soothe ourselves back to it eventually.

Being able to create our best life where we feel content, calm, and happy is totally possible by looking within ourselves at difficult times. Self-soothing is such a powerful tool when it comes to doing this. Things are going to happen that will threaten our inner peace and stability. That's just life. Things are going to try to hinder us as we attempt to bloom. Being able to soothe ourselves emotionally and mentally allows us to block those things out like a ninja and not give them the power to consume our thoughts and our feelings.

By not letting the negativity in, we can continue our journey of focusing inward to reach the best place we possibly can. Your inner peace, happiness, and well-being will become so powerful when you learn how to successfully self-soothe yourself in trying times and sticky situations. The little things won't drag you down, the conflicts won't weigh so hard on you, and you will be able to better navigate your emotions and how you respond to them. Nothing is going to be able to keep you from continuing to bloom. You're about to be unstoppable.

THINGS TO REMEMBER:

15| ACCOUNTABILITY

We've covered a ton of ideas up until this point in the book. But there is this huge, super important thing that we need to focus in on before we go off into the world on our own like a little sea turtle that hatches and crawls into the ocean (that was such a lame reference, but I'm totally leaving it in here, ha ha). Holding yourself accountable will either make you or break you in your relentless pursuit of blooming and finding your true inner happiness and peace, and it's as simple as that. You can read all the books in the world, listen to all the motivational podcasts you want, post all the bullshit inspirational Instagram quotes on your feed, and tell yourself you want to make the changes in your life every single day… but if you don't hold yourself accountable to actually DO these things, it will never really happen. You will never create your best life possible unless you actually go out there and DO IT.

I've been listening to *The 5 Second Rule* by Mel Robbins lately, and I totally have to include a little shout-out in here about the idea behind the rule and the book when it comes to holding yourself accountable. Mel tells us all about how she was in a shitty place in her life where her marriage was falling apart, she was unemployed, and her husband's business was going under. She goes on to explain that the snooze button became her secret weapon and she found it near impossible to get out of bed in the morning. She repeatedly says that there were many times that she wanted to do things differently and that she wanted to change, but every morning started out with the same multiple hits of the snooze button.

The hitting of the snooze button led to her kids missing the bus, not getting things done, and continuing the same patterns day in and day out that were all set off by how she started her day. So Mel created *The 5 Second Rule*. By counting down from five, she made herself move by the time she reached one. Don't wanna get out of bed? 5, 4, 3, 2, 1... Get up. Don't feel like working out like you said you would at 6 am? 5, 4, 3, 2, 1... Go.

The idea behind the rule is that in 5 seconds your mind will start to doubt and question things. You'll find an excuse to not do what you were going to do. You'll hesitate. You'll second guess. You'll question if things are really that important. You might even brush it off to another day or another time. You will not hold yourself accountable for whatever it is you were intending to do. But if you commit to moving, doing something, or jumping forward during those 5 seconds, odds are you're gonna do whatever it is you're questioning or thinking about. I absolutely love this idea for getting shit done!

"Parenting" is another idea I've picked up from the amazing Mel Robbins in one of her online sessions from the book. The idea behind "parenting" basically means that you will need to be the one making sure you are getting things done and following through with what you need to accomplish just like your parents would. Just like your parents would ask if you did your homework after school or if you finished your chores before dinner when you were younger, you will need to ask yourself if you've done the self-work that you need to be getting done and prioritizing.

You will need to check in with yourself regularly to make sure you are doing your own work. It may seem silly or like you shouldn't need to keep doing it repeatedly, but you absolutely do. You will need to make sure that you are doing the work that needs to be done on a regular basis. Otherwise, you may start slacking off or fall off the wagon altogether and not even realize it as its happening. You need to make sure you are holding yourself accountable to do what needs to be done.

I love both of Mel's ideas. They have stuck with me long after I heard them and I have been able to work them into my own everyday life on my pursuit of creating true inner happiness. If you haven't checked out any of her stuff yet, I highly recommend it. She is an amazing motivational speaker and really makes you understand that YOU are responsible for everything that you want to make of your life. Talk about the ultimate inspo for holding yourself accountable. Just as Mel goes over again and again in much of her work… YOU have the ability to make your life into whatever you want it to be. YOU can make things happen. YOU can make changes. YOU are in the driver's seat here.

If you want to truly change your life, nobody is going to hold your hand or hold the door open for you. Mommy and Daddy aren't going to walk you through this one. Your partner can't do this work for you. Your assistant can't cover your ass if you don't get this work done. YOU need to make the decision to actually do this. You need to show up and put in the effort to change your own life every single day. You need to make the moves. You need to shake things up. You need to just DO IT. If you fail or give up along the way, the only person you can blame will be yourself. You are the one solely responsible for knowing that you want true inner happiness and the best life possible for yourself, and that YOU can make it happen if you really want to.

It's really easy to say you're going to change and then keep doing the same things over and over again like a record stuck on repeat. I will use my drinking as a perfect example… Do you know how many times I would get absolutely shit-faced, blackout drunk and cause something negative or unpleasant to happen in my own life? There were so many times I woke up having to call or text someone to apologize for something that went down the previous night. There were also many, many "I'm sorry, I know I need to get my shit together…" texts where I very clearly knew that alcohol and partying were the complete root of the problem. I spent over a decade sending texts like these and making phone calls like these without ever changing anything. I knew exactly what the problem was, but I wasn't holding myself accountable to actually change things.

It was not until I made the conscious and deliberate effort to change my life that I actually followed through with what I had already been saying for years. Nobody was going to do the work and change my life for me…but ME. I had to finally step up, take responsibility for my life and my actions, and make something happen. I had to stop saying what I knew other people wanted to hear just to make them happy at that moment. I had to stop lying to myself (and others) by saying I was going to fix things just to turn around and do it all over again the next weekend. It had become a vicious cycle that continued because I wasn't holding myself accountable to actually do anything.

You can apply this idea of holding yourself accountable to numerous areas of your life. Wanna lose weight? Hold yourself accountable. Wanna get a better job? Hold yourself accountable. Wanna save more money? Hold yourself accountable. Wanna have a better relationship or marriage? You guessed it. Hold yourself accountable. You get the point here. By holding yourself accountable you will have to be the one to step up and do something to make the things you want to happen actually happen. You will have to be the one to make a move. You will have to be the one to get shit done. Otherwise you can keep talking about the all things you'd like to do or change in your life all you want all day long and nothing will ever change.

Obviously today we are focusing in on holding ourselves accountable to do the self-work to find true inner happiness while creating the best life for ourselves that we possibly can. But what else would you like to start holding yourself accountable for? What else would you like to step up and start changing in your life? I bet you can think of a few things right off the top of your head. You might be able to rattle off multiple things right away. If it's easier for you to focus on just one thing at a time, then absolutely do that. But if you're an overachiever like me, I prefer to tackle multiple things at once. So if you are inspired and wanting to jump right in and start changing multiple things in your life at once, by all means do it!

Right now I'm holding myself accountable to eat healthier and drop the new relationship weight I gained by eating out with my boyfriend way too often. I'm holding myself accountable to finish this book and send it off to my editor by a certain date. I'm holding myself accountable to drink more water. I'm holding myself accountable to practice exactly what I preach in this book in my own life. I'm also holding myself accountable to give myself more time to relax and not be a workaholic. As you can probably realize by my little list I threw together here, it's totally doable to tackle multiple things at once. It may sound intimidating at first, but when you break it down into a lot of little things it is much easier to take on.

One example of accountability I've been practicing in my life is with these books that I write. They are a perfect example of how I could either make them or break them, and only me. Self-publishing means just that, you're doing EVERYTHING YOURSELF. There's nobody promoting the book for you unless you get lucky and people enjoy it and share it. There's nobody offering to help you edit it unless you are paying them to do so. There's nobody posting pictures and advertising it online except for you. When you self-publish, you are solely responsible for being your book's author, the creative director, the public relations assistant, the advertising pro, the marketing master and so on and so on.

I could have half-assed my books. I could have just gotten them done quick and easy, put them online, and let Jesus take the wheel. A good amount of the beginning success I had with *Sober as F**** was because I was pushing it online, creating giveaways with signed copies, and personally requesting reviews for Amazon from people I knew. Had I not held myself accountable to make my books known and promoted them, that first book may not have done as well as it has so far. I'm sure my friends and family would have bought it to support me. I'm sure a handful of people searching for books about sobriety on Amazon may have stumbled on it. But a lot of the success that the book has had so far is because I made it happen.

The same will go for this book when it is finished and released. I'm sure my family and friends will support my work and buy it right away. Just like the first book, I'm sure that some people will stumble on it while searching for personal development books on Amazon. I know that I will have some people that have read *Sober as F**** that will purchase the book because they have felt connected to my story. But a good amount of any other interest in it initially will be because I have created it. I will be the only one helping this second book of mine take its first steps out into the world. I will be the one building it up into what it is when it is first released. I am absolutely holding myself accountable to make sure I do everything that I can on my end to make *Innerbloom* reach and help a lot of people.

Obviously, the biggest thing that I have been responsible for holding myself completely accountable for is my sobriety. Although I eventually sought out and accepted help, I had to make the initial decision to become sober from alcohol for myself. I had to decide that I was not going to say I was going to change and then not actually do anything like I had so many times in the past. Nobody else was going to be able to actually do this, but me. Sure, people could support me and tell me what they thought I should do, but ultimately I was the only one that was going to be able to make it happen. I was the only person that I could hold accountable for taking the first step into the journey of sobriety. It was me and only me doing this.

Nobody else has gotten me to the point of being two and a half years sober right now but me. I was the one that had to fight every battle, face every issue, and overcome every trying time. I was the one that had to stay strong through the depression and the tears. I was the one that had to push myself harder when it would have been much easier to just give in. I was responsible for making the intentional decision to keep going. I was the only one that could be held accountable for making this happen and for taking it as far as I'm taking it.

I'm also the only one that could use my story and my gift to share with others. I'm the only one that could use what I've gone through to try to help others going through something similar. Nobody else was going to come knock on my door asking to write a book about the hot mess, party girl from Detroit that almost died in a Detroit hospital. I held myself accountable for using my experience and find something good in it. I held myself accountable to use what happened to better the life of myself and the lives of others. And that's exactly what I'm making sure I am doing.

When you take full responsibility for being the one that needs to make things happen, it will get easier to show up and follow through. Once you can get yourself into the thought process and mindset that you are capable of doing anything you want to do or of changing anything you want to change, its kind of hard to get yourself out of it. You will realize just how much power you hold in your own life. You will realize that you literally harness everything you need to make it into exactly what you want it to be, and that might be enough right there to get the ball rolling. When you see that changes start to happen and take shape in your life because of your own deliberate thoughts or actions, you will realize just how much more you can do. Once you realize just how much you are capable of doing all by yourself, the sky will be the limit.

But, before we get carried away on another positivity rant, let's do another quick reality check and acknowledge that you're probably gonna screw this up at some point. We might as well just be honest about it. It is just plain human nature to understand that nobody is perfect, we aren't great at everything we try to do, and we mess things up from time to time. It's not the end of the world when it comes to starting your journey of finding inner happiness if you have a few slip ups. Because you're doing just that, starting it. You've taken the first steps already, which is an accomplishment in itself. You're not doomed if you don't get it perfect the first time around, because there's always another chance to keep at it.

There's always going to be more to learn, new things to try, and more ways to make your life better. The extent to which you can create a life of inner happiness and peace is endless. That is amazing if you ask me…Understanding that true inner happiness in a never-ending thing. You can always find more of it. You can always make more of it. It is absolutely limitless.

When you do mess up, do something wrong, or slip back to some Negative Nancy ways, just hold yourself accountable for it. The same way we've talked about holding yourself accountable for doing the things you need to do, hold yourself accountable for when you don't do them too. Like we've already been over many times, this whole journey and self-work thing is on you, boo. So either way, hold yourself responsible for it. You are the one making the right turn at the fork in the road, or you are also the one turning the wrong way at that same fork. Accountability goes both ways. By using it to your advantage you can bounce back from a setback and turn it into a comeback time and time again.

It's time to start holding yourself 100% accountable for the changes you are making in your life as you finish the last few chapters of this book. You may have started making some of the changes along the way already, and that is amazing! Good for you for jumping right in and getting started with no hesitation. If you are waiting until you finish the book to start making the changes to turn your days into this new, positive, and happy lifestyle, kudos to you too!

You picked up this book. You started reading it. You're still reading it. What all of this means is that you know what you want for your life. You know that you want better. And you know that you deserve it. Either way, let's talk about how we can make sure we are holding ourselves accountable for following through with things long after you turn the last page, close the cover, and put this book up on the bookshelf.

Really read each chapter and look at your own life. Look at your own ways. Reflect. Look at your own habits. Look at the way you live. Look at your past. Look at your present. Notice the things you need to change more. I included the lined pages so you could take notes and highlight big ideas. I wanted to make sure you would be able to return back to them as notes for guidance or a refresher along the way. Keep revisiting the areas you struggle with. Acknowledge the areas you have been successful at making changes in. If you find an area you are struggling to make changes in, keep trying. Keep approaching it from a new direction. Keep at it. Don't give up if at first you don't get it just right. Keep trying until you get it.

Try to approach everyday moments and situations with these ideas we have gone over in the back of your mind. Try to be a little more intentional when you are applying the changes whenever you can. If you really do the work, it will work. You will be able to turn this life into one that is full of happiness, peace, and love. You will be able to feel yourself innerblooming day in and day out. You will able to create the best life possible for yourself. Always remember that YOU have the ability to turn this life into whatever you want it to be. No matter how many hardships you face, no matter how many obstacles are in your way, and no matter how hard it might be.

The bottom line is… you bought this book and you started reading it. You had the intention or the thought at some point that there are things about your life that you want to change for the better. You had the thought that you wanted to change your life to turn it into the best one possible. Well, guess what? Simply buying a book and reading it isn't going to make shit happen. It's the first step, that's for sure. But if you finish these pages, close this book, and put in up on the shelf without making any actual, intentional changes in your own life… absolutely nothing will change. You are solely responsible for using what we learn here and applying it to your life. You are the only one that can be held accountable for taking action and making your life into the best life possible. It's all on YOU, boo boo. Let's make it happen.

THINGS TO REMEMBER:

16 | NEW YOU

So as you move forward from this whole journey of looking inward to find true inner happiness in your life, I'd like to elaborate a little bit more how important it is to not close this book once you finish it, throw it to the side, and completely forget everything that we just went over here. Old habits die hard, and I think we can all attest to that idea. It would be easy to forget everything we just learned and slip back into our old ways. But not this time, honey. The point of this book is to learn a whole new way of living your life. A way of life that totally and completely is all about YOU and your well-being in a completely positive, unselfish way. I call it unselfish because it is not selfish at all to want the best for yourself. And odds are, it will not only better your life, but it will rub off on those around you as well. You can bet on it that they are going to be loving these new positive changes you have made in your life! You may even inspire them to make some changes in their own lives too, which is amazing! So now it's time to practice what we have just preached. We're taking the training wheels off of the bike, and it's time to start pedaling all on our own now.

If you need to do some things to give yourself daily reminders to continue looking inward and practicing living in a way that reflects your new inner happiness and growth, do it! Start saying a morning mantra such as "I have everything I need within me." Leave yourself a brightly colored post-it note on the mirror to read while you brush your teeth with a subtle reminder that "you are beautiful". Meal prep your meals in advance so you have a little bit of homemade self-love to take to work with you to nourish your body on your lunch break or on the go. Keep a self-development book on your nightstand to do a little self-work every night before bed. There can be a million other simple, tiny ways to remind yourself to continue practicing this act of looking inward and keeping the positivity and happiness alive and well. These are just a few simple suggestions of mine, but totally find your own! See what works for you and your daily routine, and work it!

As I've gone over and over again, relapsing to old ways is an extremely common part of anyone's making a dramatic change in their life, so don't beat yourself up if you catch yourself resorting to your old ways. Don't be surprised if there are times you mindlessly resort to looking to outward things for the quick and easy answers because it's probably going to happen. Of course it is easy and comfortable to go with the things we already know. Going with things that are new and different can be a challenge. It can be scary. It can be uncomfortable. But as we've seen in a million motivational quote posts, AMAZING things happen outside of your comfort zone. And we are totally getting out of ours.

So don't give up completely if you slip into your old mindset from time to time. It happens, so we just need to practice getting back on track with our new ways. It's going to take intentional living. It's going to require intention in your everyday life and everyday decisions. We're making big changes to upgrade and up-level the way we live our lives. Change takes time, and if you put the time into this change it will truly shift everything.

It took me a long time and a lot of relapsing to my old ways to get here. Trust me, it was not pretty. You'd think that every time I resorted to my old ways and ended up feeling depressed, unworthy, and unfulfilled I would have caught on sooner. God only knows how many times I've had to resort to my old ways with men to realize that every single time it only led to myself in tears with a pint of Halo Top ice cream on a Saturday night. So when I say don't beat yourself up over resorting to your old ways, I mean it. Some of us are stubborn and it just takes us a little bit longer to accept things and live in a new way. Some of us have to learn things the hard way, and I was definitely one of them.

It's normal to take time to adjust to a new way of living. I'm writing a freakin' book about it and I've screwed it up enough times along the way myself to know that. But you learn as you go and you learn from your f*** ups. So give it time. The number of empty pints of Halo Top ice cream I went through in the past year or so speak for themselves. Okay, so let's not kid ourselves, the Halo Top is still fully stocked in the freezer. But now I enjoy it on any given day as a treat with my loving boyfriend, not because David with the tattoos, muscles, and awesome beard from Tinder turned out to be a total asshole (surprise, surprise).

Just wait until you start to feel the amazing shift in your life when you truly start working on creating your own true and authentic happiness. Wait until you feel what it is like to truly bloom inside. You're going to be so hungry for so much more of it once you experience what it can feel like. You are going to be on a relentless pursuit to find as much of it as you can. Be selfish here. Find and take as much of it as you can because it is all there for your taking.

I find this new life indescribable at times. I can't pinpoint the exact moment it completely shifted for me, but one day I just realized that everything felt new. Things just felt better. I smiled more. I laughed more. I wasn't dreading the day when I woke up in the morning, and I wasn't watching the clock waiting for it to be over in the afternoon. I enjoyed my time with the people in my life more. I created things in my life to look forward to. I had more confidence in myself. I was more successful. I was living the best life I had ever lived, and I am still living it everyday.

The list of the ways that my life got better when I worked to find true inner happiness is never ending. I don't think it will ever end really, which is amazing to think about! I am constantly seeing the effects that the changes in my life have made on everything I do now. It has truly shown me that I am in control of my life and the way I live it. I am capable of finding my own inner peace and happiness no matter what life may throw at me along the way. I am always capable of living my best life possible, no matter what.

The changes I've made by looking inward and doing the self-work have transformed my life into a daily experience of serenity, happiness, and a calmer outlook on absolutely everything. I can confidently say that the sense of calmness is definitely the most noticeable shift I have felt in myself. I used to feel like I constantly had a million things to do or like I had to be working on something constantly to feel fulfilled. Now I am actually able to give myself an entire evening off without feeling lazy or guilty about it. This alone has totally changed everything. We need time to shut off and recharge. We need to make time to take care of ourselves and our well-being. By accepting and practicing this idea, the benefits I have seen in my life have been absolutely unreal. I definitely don't plan on going back to my old ways anytime soon now that I have seen what this new approach to life can feel like on a daily basis.

Just wait until you see how your newfound happiness and lifestyle starts to encourage those around you to do the same. When people start to see how you are just oozing a sense of happiness and being at peace with your life like never before, they are going to want it too. They are going to keep trying to figure out what's different about you. Rebecca at work might ask "Did you do something different with your hair?" Don't be surprised if everyone starts asking if you lost weight, if you met someone, or what's gotten into you (in a good way). When you feel good on the inside it shows on the outside. Everyone is going to be able to see your inner happiness on the outside of the new you.

We all know that we can see Debbie Downer from a mile away with her perma-frown wrinkling her mid-30s skin. She just looks down. She looks sad. She looked like she is just going through the motions. You know when something is bothering her, even if she tries her hardest to hide it. Most of the time we can tell that something isn't right with Debbie. But we can all also see Positive Patty with her beaming smile and lightness in her step from a mile away. We all want to be like Patty. Her life just looks so easy, breezy, and wonderful. Patty just seems to have it all figured out. We all wonder how Patty is always so happy and why the sun always seems to be shining out of her ass, and the new you may be turning into Patty. BE PATTY.

So let the sun shine out of your ass. Let others see this new you, smiling and walking with a new sense of lightness. Odds are, they will want it to. And they might even ask you how you found it. I'll just casually mention here that I wouldn't be mad if you passed the name of this book along to them (I hope you like that shameless self-promoting I just did there). Who knows, maybe we could even start a revolution of people looking inward and doing the work to find their most authentic true inner happiness. Maybe we could help women everywhere to create the best life of their wildest dreams. Maybe we could help women everywhere feel what it is like to innerbloom.

I think it would do everyone a bit of good to do this in today's day and age. We waste so much time and energy in the world on negativity and drama. Although I watch the news to keep on top of what's going on in the world, it can be truly depressing to watch it at times. There are so many horrible things happening in the world today that get plastered all over the media. I think it would be amazing to add a little bit of lightness to all of our lives to help block some of it out.

So, this is where you get to go out into the world and start practicing everything we've just learned Take your notes and take the ideas that really stood out to you. You have so much knowledge and information right now that you can begin to infuse into your new life. Start making little changes in your everyday life and watch those small changes turn into much bigger changes with time.

Live each day intentionally and with this whole idea of innerblooming fresh in your mind. Make every decision with the goal of creating the best life you can possible dream up in your pretty little head. The idea here is that the life of your dreams, the life that you visualize and strive for should be the life you are creating. Whatever that may look like to you when you visualize it, that is what you should be working towards. Work each and every day to make yours start to resemble it a little bit more. Day by day, change by change, and shift by shift.

I can't tell you how many times people have commented on how happy I look now. It shows in everything that I do that I have true inner and authentic happiness because of the new life I have created for myself. It really is a completely new me. I can't even describe to you how grateful I feel at times that I have gotten here. Sometimes when I stop at random times in my day and realize how much happier and more amazing my life is now, it almost brings me to tears. It gives me such an overwhelming feeling of plain old gratitude. I feel so lucky, so blessed, and like I am in full bloom as this new woman in this new life of mine.

I'm getting to the point that when I look back and reflect on how far I've come, I don't even know who that girl from the past is anymore. I don't even know whose life that was anymore. You will get to this point too. Once you begin living this new way of life, the ways of your past will seem like a distant memory. You might even start to feel like I do now, where my old life has become almost foreign to me. The old you will become almost unrecognizable to the powerful, positive force you will transform into. Your old life will look foreign to the new upgraded life you will be living now. It will be SUCH a beautiful thing to see and to feel.

Imagine looking back and being able to see the changes that you have made. Imagine how incredible it will feel to know that YOU and

ONLY YOU made all of it happen. Imagine looking back and seeing how much you have grown as a person. Imagine how amazing it will be to know that you did the work and made the changes to make all of it possible. It was all because of YOU. How incredible, amazing, and empowering is that!? Knowing that everything about this new you, this happy, positive, and powerful new you, exists solely because YOU made an intentional decision and did the work to make it happen. Knowing that this new life, the best life you could have possibly created for yourself, exists only because YOU created it. It's time for you to feel all of this.

It's time to bloom.

THINGS TO REMEMBER:

EPILOGUE

Here we are at the end of book number two. Never in my wildest dreams did I see myself here... Self-publishing my second book before I even hit my three year anniversary of sobriety. And let me tell you, I'm only just getting started with the big dreams and goals I am setting out for myself. It just goes to show how much you can truly transform your life into one that is a picture of your wildest dreams (or dreams you didn't even know you had yet). I was able to change my life from a never-ending party and emotional disaster into an incredible life that blooms over and over again with strength, beauty, and true inner happiness. It was all possible because I made the intentional decision to do it, and because I followed through with it.

If you want proof that changing your life into that of your wildest dreams is possible, well look no further than here. I was a lost young woman for a very long time. I was relying on superficial and outside things and people in my life to dictate who I was, how I felt, and how I lived. I was also allowing these things to dictate my happiness in life. The truth was that I had everything within myself all along that I needed to be truly happy, I just wasn't aware of it yet. It took a long time, some serious growing up, and a big, life changing event to really open my eyes and show me that I had it all along.

I will forever credit everything that I have been able to do with shifting my life to the day that changed everything... the day that I shouldn't have made it. It was on that day that I vowed to God, the Universe, and any other higher power that might be out there that I would change, and I did. I promised myself that with this second chance at life I would live every day to its full extent from that day forward… live in every moment, take every chance, love as freely as possible, and not waste a second of my life ever again not feeling gratitude and purpose.

Being able to share my life experiences with the world has been the most humbling thing I've ever done. Reading emails and messages from people around the world who have read my work and relate to my story is absolutely unreal. Knowing that there are a lot of people out there going through the same things I went through and feeling the same ways I did is extremely reassuring. Knowing that people are connecting with my story and my words just continues to give me constant reassurance that THIS is my gift, THIS is my path, and THIS is my purpose. THIS is exactly where I am supposed to be. THIS is exactly what I am supposed to be doing.

The way that I rebuilt my life after my first year of sobriety and beyond has been something I have held very close to my heart. I feel very lucky that I had the second chance to do it. It was not always easy and there were plenty of low points, but now I see that they were all worth it. They were worth it because what they gave me was the experiences and knowledge that I can now share with others. I can share these things with others to help them in their own journey, and I feel so humbled that I am able to do that. Feeling this way and being lucky enough to live this new life that I love makes all of it worth it.

Why not today? Why not now? Why not everyday? You have the full potential to turn every day into one that is exactly what you want it to be. You have the opportunity to create your best life… one that is full of the most true and authentic inner happiness possible. That is the beautiful thing about your life, that it is like an open book with empty pages just waiting to be written on. Start writing the story of what you want your life to be.

I'm so excited for all of you to have the knowledge and the inspiration to create your best life possible. I can't wait for each and every one of you to feel yourself truly live and bloom from the inside. It is such an amazing gift to feel this way each day, and I can't wait to pass that gift onto you.

I hope that from this day forward that you live each day with intention and purpose. I hope that you begin to rewrite your own story into one that you love to share with others. I hope that you wake up each day feeling grateful to be alive. I hope that you live each day ready to make it another one of the best days of your life. I hope that you find true and lasting love. I hope that you purge your life of the things that you do not need anymore. I hope that you find what makes you come alive. I hope that you will transform your life into everything that you want it to be…

I hope you bloom.

xx .

P.S. I love seeing your screenshots and photos of my books! Seeing my baby out in the world and in the hands of so many real and amazing people makes my heart skip a beat. Make sure you tag me on social media and #INNERBLOOM when you share!

(All my social media pages are on the About the Author page, so come say hi! :))

BIG THANKS

To the person or people I will most likely forget to thank, thank you.

To my mama, I can still never thank you enough for everything you do and are for me. You are still (and will always be) my absolute best friend. Thank you for always supporting me in everything that I do, including handing out multiple business cards and books at your workplace whenever you have the opportunity to do so (ha ha). I love you for everything, Ter Bear.

To the rest of my family, I know you sometimes think I am out of my mind when I have these big, crazy dreams and goals for myself. Thank you for being open to all of the ideas I have and the life that I have created for myself.

To my girl gang, you know who all of you are! I would take up far too many pages thanking each of you personally, but thank you to each and every one of you for being the greatest girlfriends and my biggest supporters. Thank you to my life-long friends, my new friends, my online friends, and everyone in between. You are such a source of empowerment and encouragement no matter what my big, crazy ideas are. I have so much love for you guys.

Andrew… I can't thank you enough for changing my whole outlook and view of what love is. You have been my biggest supporter throughout my finishing this book. You have been my best friend since the day that I met you. You are my rock. You are my partner in crime. I love you for all that you are and for all that you encourage me to be. Basically, I just freakin' love you.

To my Sarah, we laughed so much about your wanting your name being in both of my books while on our girl's weekend trip to Toronto that I couldn't not name drop you in this book. So here it is. Here I am, "Just living my best life…" (LOL)

To my therapist Debbie, thank you for asking me every single week "So, how's Innerbloom?" As silly as it sounds, telling you what I had done for the book every week made me feel even more excited about finishing this project. Thank you for getting me to where I am today… happy and healthy.

To Cara Lockwood and Caroline Johnson, thank you for always making my ideas come to life in both of my books now! After such an amazing first book editing and cover work, it was only right to make you both a part of this project too.

To YOU. Thank you so much for continuing to support my crazy dreams. It's unreal to think that I spent months on this book and now it is a real thing in your hands. You are reading the words of my life and my story. You are making my wildest dreams of being a self-published author come true. You still the real MVP.

ABOUT THE AUTHOR

As an entrepreneur, makeup artist, YouTuber, and blogger, Sarah Ordo is your not-so-average female Millennial craving to leave her mark on this world in more ways than one. Her award-winning on location hair and makeup company (based out of Metro Detroit), 24Luxe Hair & Makeup, has been making clients and brides look stunning for their special occasions since 2013. Her YouTube channel and Instagram page reach thousands of her followers daily featuring a variety of beauty, health, lifestyle, and wellness posts and videos. Her Youtube videos documenting and following her sobriety have reached thousands of viewers internationally, and have even been featured on *Dateline NBC*.

Sarah has been featured on and interviewed for numerous blogs and podcasts including Cara Alwill Leyba's *Style Your Mind* Podcast and Courtney Bentley's *Fit Fierce & Fabulous* Podcast.

On her webiste, *sarahordo.com,* Sarah blogs about living sober, self-love, mental health, and many other raw, honest topics. She also features reviews of the newest beauty, health, & lifestyle products and trends.

Sober as F*** is the first full-length memoir and book written by Sarah, which was released in May 2017. *Innerbloom* is her second full-length book, which is a personal development/memoir hybrid following how she rebuilt her life during her journey in sobriety and beyond.

Follow Sarah:
www.sarahordo.com
Youtube: Sarah Ordo
Instagram: @24Luxe_Sarah

Made in the USA
Middletown, DE
11 September 2018